THE
RIVER
CAFE
LOOK
BOOK

THE RIVER CAFE LOOK BOOK

RUTH ROGERS
SIAN WYN OWEN
JOSEPH TRIVELLI
MATTHEW DONALDSON

This book is
dedicated to
Richard Rogers
who taught us
to look.

The first pages of this book are simply photographs of recipes we have chosen. Next to them are images which speak to them, whether in shape, colour or texture.

A vase of dramatically wilting tulips set next to spaghetti alle vongole – and we recognize the shared curves and complex and graceful warp of stalk in the pasta.

Roasted triangles of red and yellow peppers soften opposite a floppy straw hat, folded into a box.

We want these connections to give you a story to be found, a mystery to be solved. Cooking is more than just science, rigorous and measured.

It is also art – a picture on a plate. Cooking involves all of your senses. Above all, it involves your imagination.

LOOK

Pizza Margherita 118

Broad Bean Bruschetta 120

Spinach and Prosciutto Frittata 122

RAP

Pizza with Taleggio, Potato and Thyme 124

Focaccia 126

Mozzarella with Roasted Cherry Tomatoes 128

MI
MI 9T3134

Fusilli with Zucchini 132

Spaghetti alle Vongole 134

V

Penne all'Amatriciana 136

Spaghetti Lemon 138

Risotto with Tomato and Basil 140

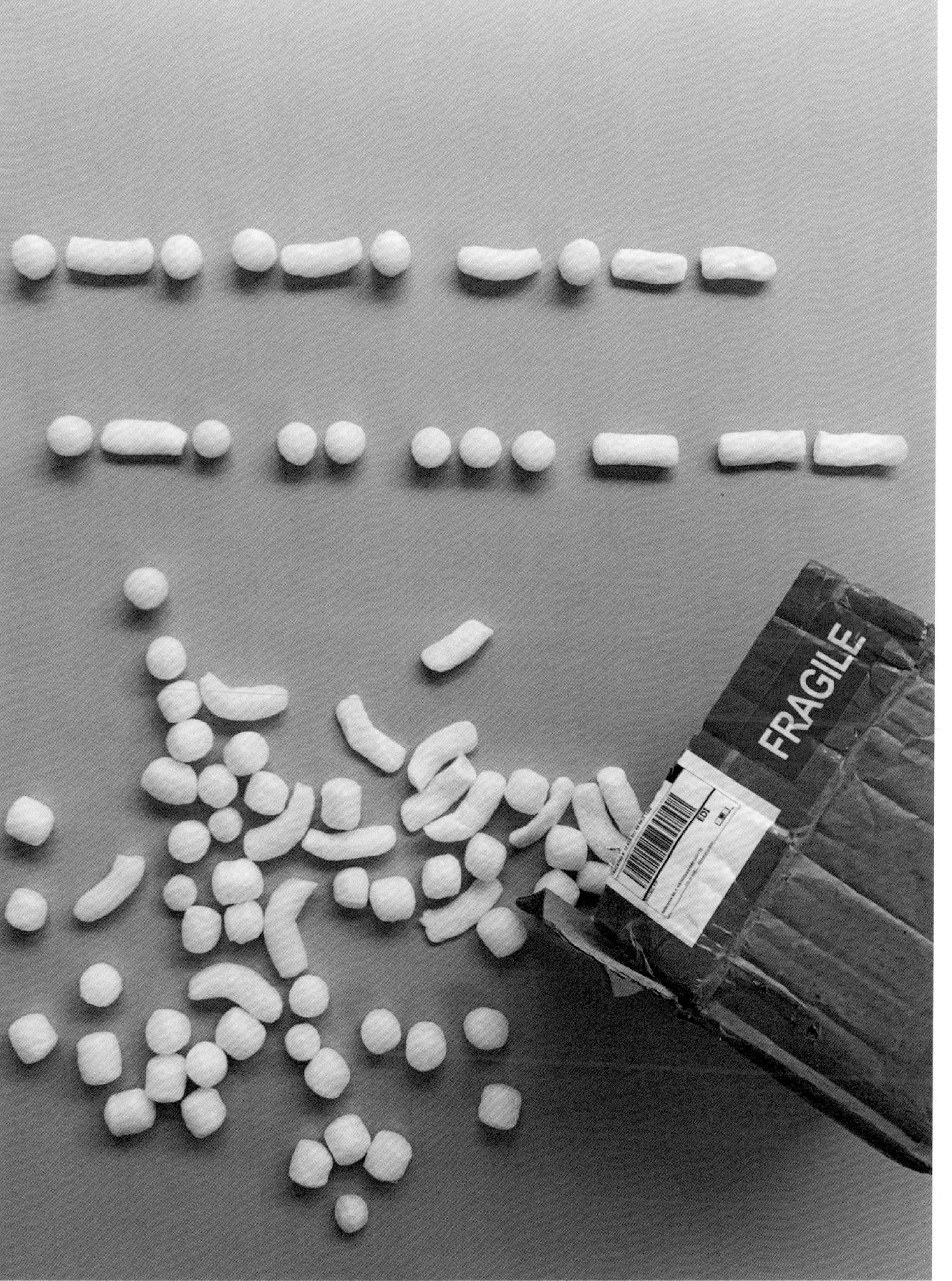
FRAGILE

1
6

Casarecce with Pesto 142

Cacio e Pepe 144

Rigatoni with Pork Ragu 146

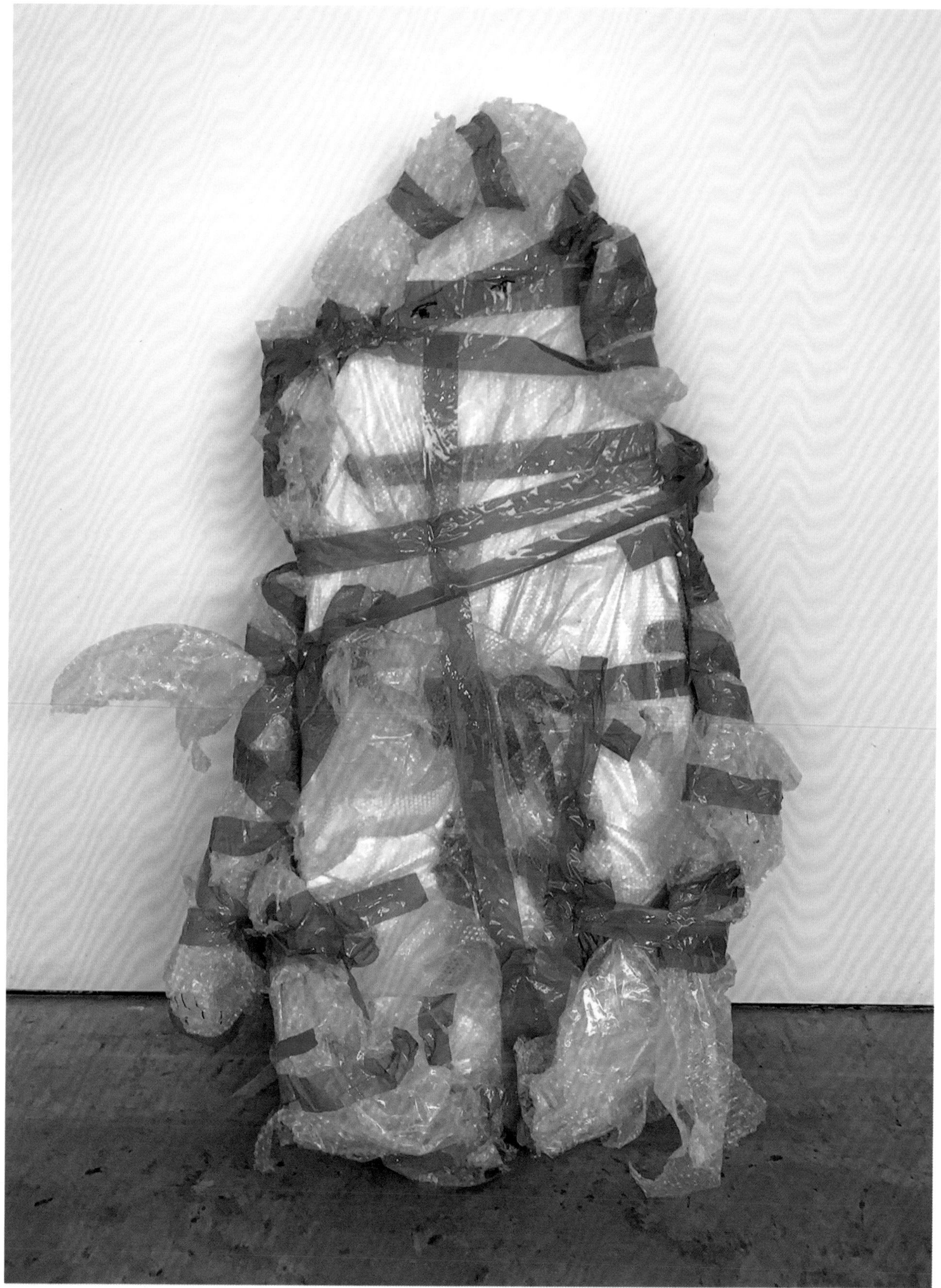

Spaghetti with Peas and Prosciutto 148

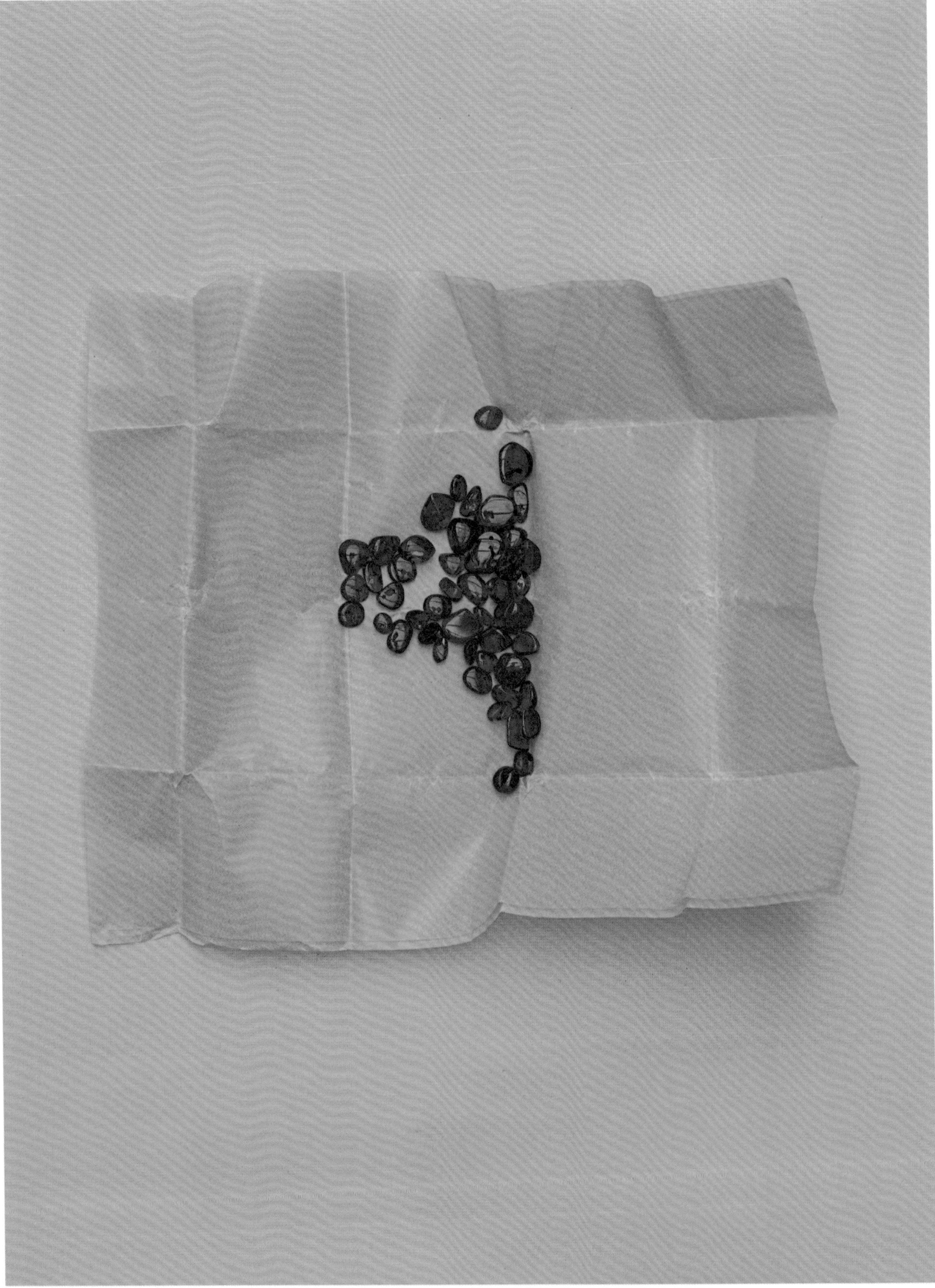

Penne with Quick Sausage Sauce 152

SPECIALIST
INGENIOUS
BLEND

Gnocchi with Tomato Sauce 154

CONTROL SPEED • ECO

Pappa al Pomodoro 160

Chicken Soup 162

Smashed Potatoes with Green Beans 166

Zucchini Salad 170

Zucchini Trifolati 172

Slow-Roasted Tomatoes with Basil 174

Slow-Cooked Peas 176

AUTO-ECOLE

Green Beans in Tomato 178

Roasted Vegetables 180

Roasted Red and Yellow Peppers 182

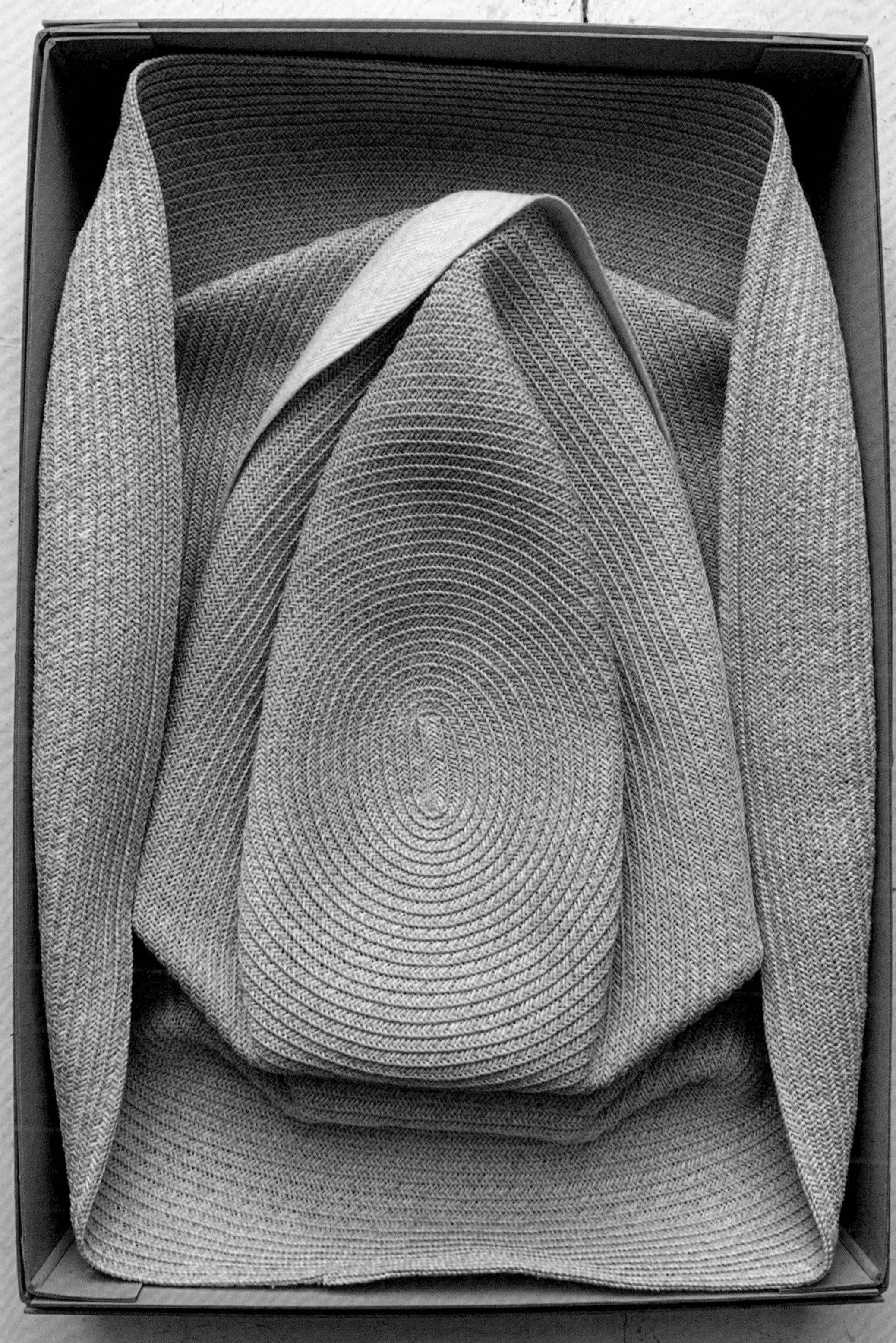

Roasted Datterini Tomatoes 184

Tuscan Roasted Potatoes 186

Rainbow

Roasted Potatoes with Lemon and Thyme 188

Stuffed Squash 190

Sea Bass Over Potatoes 194

Spiedini of Monkfish and Scallops 196

Monkfish Wrapped in Pancetta 198

Spatchcock Chicken in Milk 202

Beaten Lamb Cutlets 204

STOP

Arista Di Maiale 208

Almond Meringue with Strawberries 212

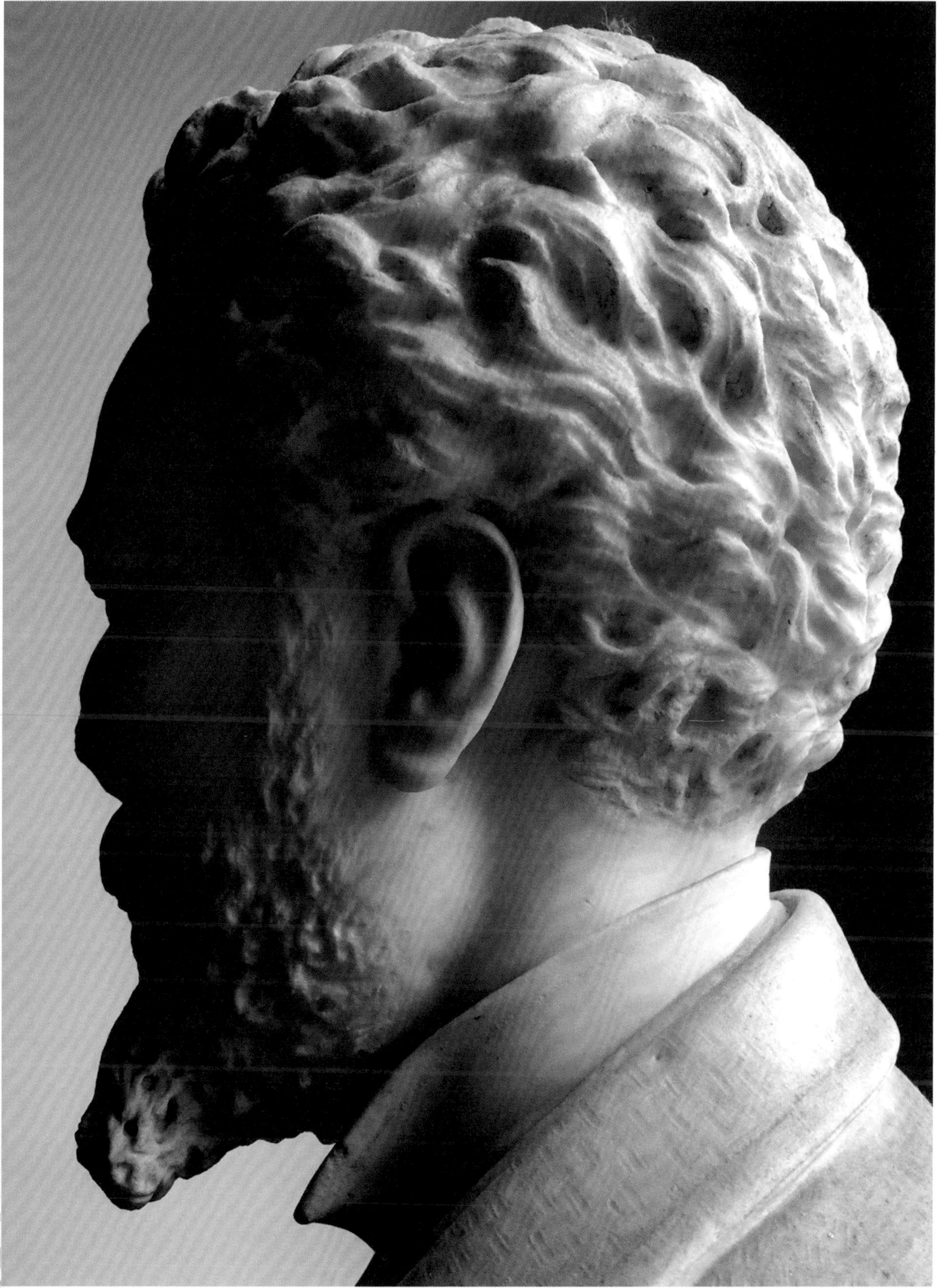

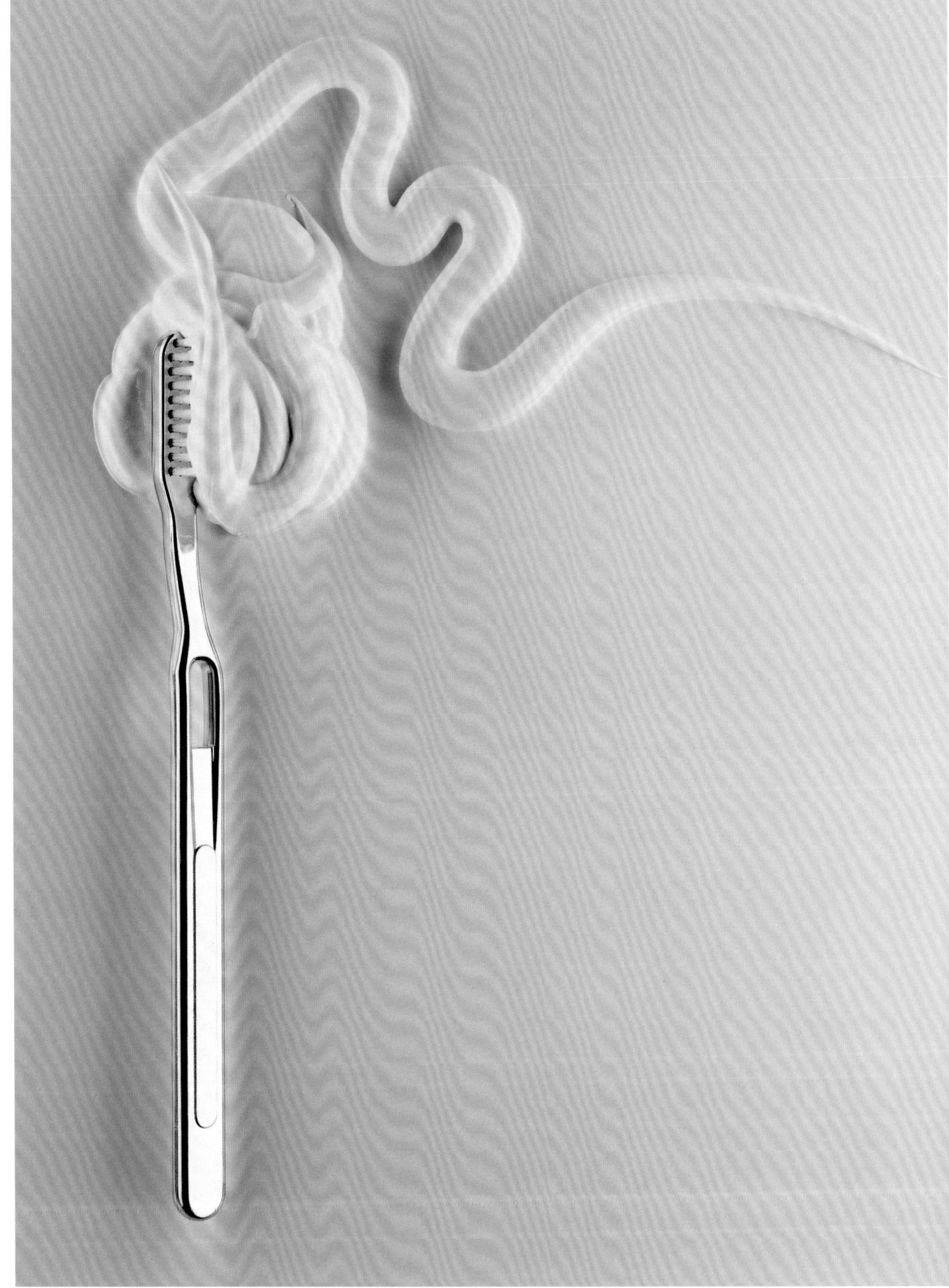

Lemon Ice Cream 214

EMERGENCY CALLS
FOR
FIRE
POLICE
AMBULANCE
999
TUV
WXY
OQ

Raspberry Sorbet 216

Hazelnut Praline Semifreddo 218

Pressed Chocolate Cake 220

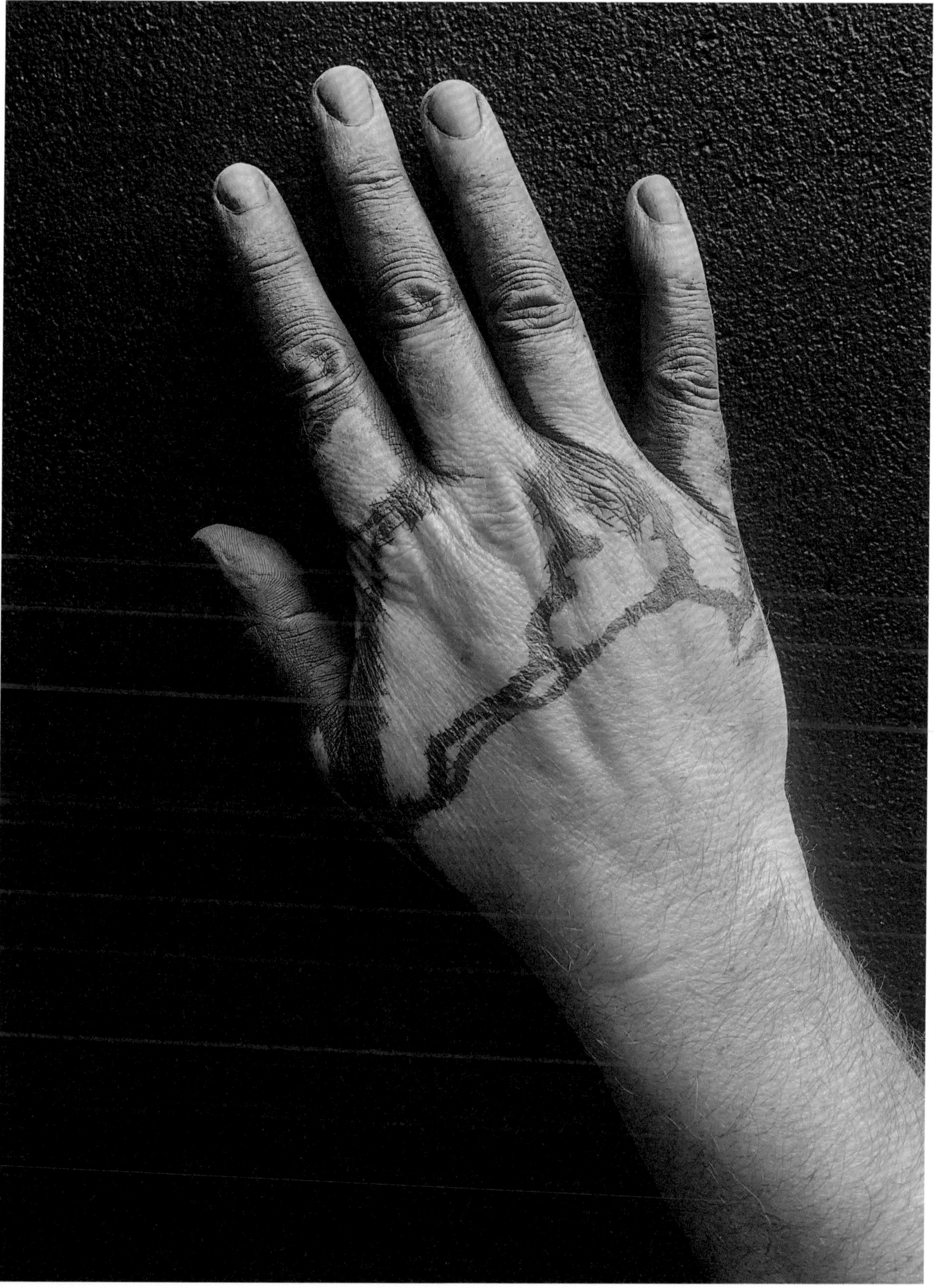

Crostata 222

Chocolate Truffles 224

Pear and Almond Tart 228

Ricciarelli 230

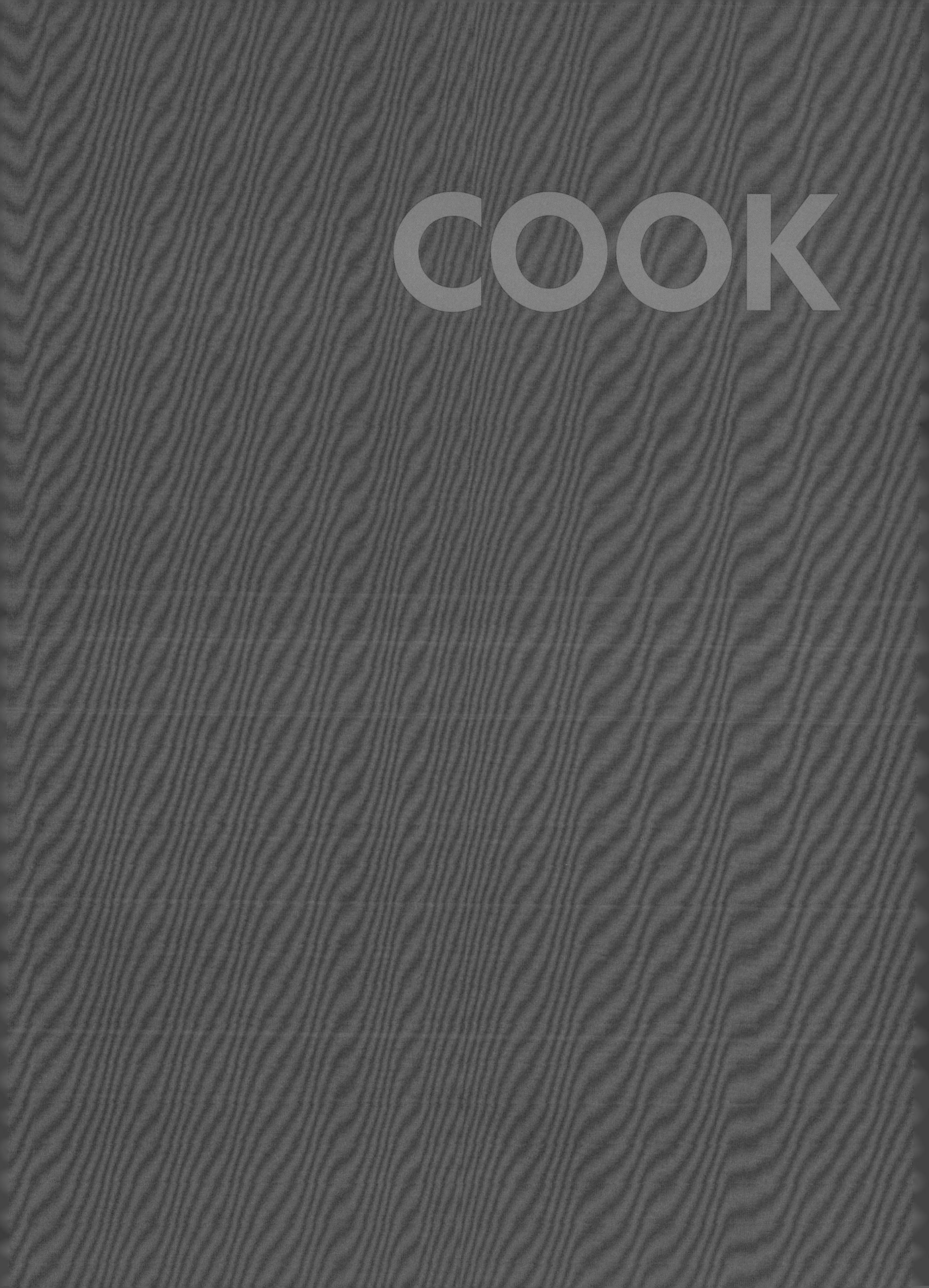
COOK

1. Begin by reading the recipe twice. The more you cook, the more you will learn about how recipes work. Don't be disheartened by your mistakes and enjoy the learning process.
2. Enjoy the process of cleaning up and keeping organized as you go.
3. Be sure the counter top and chopping boards are clean. Place a damp kitchen cloth under your chopping board to stop it sliding.
4. Organize the ingredients and equipment you will need – this is your cooking station. As chefs, we are lost without a pair of tongs on hand and recommend that you have some nearby, as well as a cloth for wiping.
5. If you're a child, ask an adult for help cutting, chopping, slicing and dicing. A sharp knife is an essential tool. Knowing how to use it safely is crucial. When things are hot, whether in a pan, grill, boiling water or baking in the oven, take great care.
6. Put your apron on and wash your hands, now you're ready.

BEGIN

ANTIPASTI

PIZZA MARGHERITA

Ingredients:

8g (2½ teaspoons) fresh yeast
or 1 sachet of dried yeast
700ml (24 fl oz/scant 3 cups)
lukewarm water
1kg (9 cups) 00 flour,
plus extra for dusting
20g (1½ tablespoons) salt,
plus extra for seasoning
1 tablespoon olive oil,
plus extrafor greasing
400g (14 oz) tin plum tomatoes
freshly ground black pepper
500g (1lb 2 oz) mozzarella,
torn into small pieces
8 basil leaves

Makes enough for 8 mini pizzas

Equipment:

scale
measuring cups
measuring spoons
tin opener
large bowl
whisk
kitchen (dish) towel
3-4 rimmed baking sheets
kitchen scissors
rolling pin
jug
baking parchment
food processor

Tear the mozzarella into small pieces so that it melts evenly.

1. In a jug, whisk the yeast into the water, then leave for 5 minutes.
2. In a large bowl, mix together the flour and salt with your hands.
3. Whisk the water and yeast again, then pour into the flour. Mix together to form a dough.
4. Cover and leave at room temperature until doubled in size.
5. Using kitchen scissors, carefully cut the dough into 150g (5½ oz) portions (about 8 balls).
6. Flip and roll with your hands to form smooth dough balls.
7. Put each ball onto floured baking sheets, cover with a kitchen (dish) towel and leave at room temperature for 1 hour.
8. While the dough is rising, put the tin of tomatoes in a food processor with a tablespoon of olive oil and season with salt and pepper. Process to a purée.
9. Put a baking sheet in the oven and preheat to 230°C/Gas Mark 8 (450°F).
10. Using a rolling pin, roll out each ball on a floured work counter with light, quick motions. Try to roll the dough as thinly as possible.
11. Place each pizzetta on the baking paper. Top with tomato, scatter the mozzarella over each pizzetta and garnish with a leaf of basil.
12. One at a time, put the pizzetta on the baking paper onto the hot baking sheet.
13. Bake in the oven on top of the preheated sheet for 6–8 minutes until the pizzetta is puffed and golden. Remove the pizzetta from the oven and repeat with the remaining pizzettas.

Photo Page 11

BROAD BEAN BRUSCHETTA

Ingredients:

300g (2½ cups) podded (shelled) broad (fava) beans
100ml (3½ fl oz/scant ½ cup) extra-virgin olive oil, plus extra for drizzling
150g (2 cups) freshly grated Parmesan
10 basil leaves
10 mint leaves
1½ cloves garlic (divided)
sea salt and freshly ground black pepper
juice of ½ lemon
4 slices sourdough bread

Serves 6

Equipment:

scale
measuring cups
measuring spoons
grater
sharp knife
blender
griddle (grill) pan (optional)

Make this with the first broad beans of the year, when they are small and sweet.

1. Put the beans in a blender with the olive oil, Parmesan, basil, mint and the ½ clove of garlic, then roughly purée.
2. Season with salt and pepper, then add lemon juice.
3. Grill the bread under the grill (broiler) or in a griddle (grill) pan over a medium heat on both sides until browned.
4. Rub the bruschetta generously with the whole clove of garlic and drizzle with a little olive oil.
5. Spread the purée on top of the bruschetta.

Photo Page 12

SPINACH AND PROSCIUTTO FRITTATA

Ingredients:

500g (1 lb 2 oz) spinach,
tough stalks removed
sea salt and freshly ground
black pepper
50g (3½ tablespoons) butter (divided)
4 large (extra-large) eggs
100g (1½ cups) freshly grated
Parmesan (divided)
2 tablespoons olive oil
4 large slices prosciutto

Serves 6

Equipment:

scale
measuring cups
measuring spoons
sharp knife
grater
large saucepan
colander
2 bowls
spoon
fork
large ovenproof frying pan
spatula
oven gloves

Once you've mastered one frittata, you can try many seasonal variations: tomato and zucchini (courgette) in the summer, spinach and Parmesan in the winter, asparagus in the spring and mushrooms in the autumn.

1. Preheat the oven to 230°C/Gas Mark 8 (450°F).
2. Bring a large saucepan of salted water to the boil.
3. Add the spinach to the pan and boil for 2 minutes.
4. Drain the spinach in a colander.
5. Put the spinach in a bowl and season with salt and pepper.
6. Mix in half the butter with a spoon.
7. Leave to cool.
8. Break the eggs into another bowl and lightly beat with a fork.
9. Stir in the spinach and half the Parmesan, then season with salt and pepper.
10. Heat the olive oil in a large frying pan over a medium heat, carefully tilting the pan to coat the entire surface.
11. Add the egg mixture and reduce the heat.
12. Cook, loosening the side from time to time with a spatula, until just set.
13. Scatter over the remaining Parmesan and knobs of butter.
14. Bake in the oven for 1–2 minutes until it rises and the edges are crisp.
15. Carefully remove the frittata from the oven using oven gloves.
16. Loosen the frittata from the pan with a spatula.
17. Turn onto a warm plate and top with prosciutto.

Photo Page 14

PIZZA WITH TALEGGIO, POTATO AND THYME

Ingredients:

Dough (see page 118)
00 flour, for dusting
salt and freshly ground black pepper
olive oil, for drizzling

Toppings
2 potatoes
400g (14 oz) taleggio, sliced
thyme

Makes enough for 8 mini pizzas

Equipment:

scale
measuring cups
measuring spoons
baking sheet
vegetable peeler
sharp knife
large saucepan
colander
rolling pin
baking (parchment) paper
oven gloves

A pizza bianca is a pizza without tomato. We like it simple, but if you want to add something salty, we often add black olives, anchovies or capers.

1. Preheat the oven to 230°C/Gas Mark 8 (450°F) for 30 minutes before baking.
2. Put a large baking sheet in the oven to heat up.
3. Bring a large saucepan of salted water to the boil.
4. Peel the potatoes and slice into thin 5-mm (¼-inch) slices.
5. Add the potatoes to the pan and boil for 1 minute, then drain in a colander.
6. Divide dough into 8 pieces.
7. Dust a work counter with flour.
8. Using a rolling pin, roll a ball on the floured counter in quick light motions.
9. Roll dough as thinly as possible and place the pizzetta on a piece of baking (parchment) paper, top with potato slices and taleggio.
10. Season with salt, pepper and thyme, then drizzle with a little olive oil.
11. Transfer the baking paper with the pizzetta to the hot baking sheet.
12. Bake for 6–8 minutes until the pizzetta is puffed and golden.
13. Carefully remove from the oven. Repeat with the remaining pizzettas.

Photo Page 16

FOCACCIA

Ingredients:

8g (2½ teaspoons) fresh yeast or
1 sachet of dried yeast
735ml (25 fl oz/3 cups) lukewarm water
1kg (9 cups) 00 flour
20g (1½ tablespoons) sea salt, plus extra for brushing and drizzling
4 tablespoons olive oil,
plus extra for brushing and drizzling

Serves 10

Equipment:

scale
measuring cups
measuring spoons
jug
whisk
large bowl
spatula
pastry brush
baking sheet
oven gloves

Focaccia is best fresh, serve it right away.

1. In a jug, whisk the yeast into the water, then leave for 5 minutes.
2. In a large bowl, mix together the flour and salt.
3. Add the olive oil to the water and yeast, then mix well.
4. Pour the wet ingredients into the dry.
5. Mix with a spatula or your hands until a shaggy dough comes together and no dry bits are left.
6. Cover with a damp kitchen (dish) towel and leave until doubled in size.
7. Generously oil a large, rimmed baking sheet.
8. With wet hands, lift the dough from the bowl and fold it over itself once or twice.
9. Carefully put the dough onto the baking sheet with the smooth side up.
10. Drizzle with olive oil, then spread it over the surface with your hands.
11. Leave to rise for 1 hour 30 minutes, gently stretching the dough every 30 minutes.
12. When the dough has nearly doubled in size and retains a finger mark when poked, wet your fingers and gently poke dimples into the dough.
13. About 30 minutes before baking, preheat the oven to 230°C/Gas Mark 8 (450°F).
14. Sprinkle the focaccia with the sea salt and drizzle with more olive oil.
15. Bake in the oven for 20–30 minutes until golden.
16. Carefully remove from the oven, then drizzle with more olive oil.
17. Slice into squares.

Photo Page 19

MOZZARELLA WITH ROASTED CHERRY TOMATOES

Ingredients:

600g (4 cups) cherry tomatoes
20 basil leaves
4 cloves garlic, halved lengthways
3 tablespoons extra-virgin olive oil,
plus extra for drizzling
sea salt and freshly ground black pepper
4 slices bread (optional)
2 large mozzarella balls (about 250g/9 oz)

Serves 4

Equipment:

scale
measuring cups
measuring spoons
sharp knife
toothpick
bowl
wooden spoon
baking dish
griddle (grill) pan (optional)
oven gloves

When you only have a handful of ingredients, the quality of those ingredients is important. The star of this salad is the cheese. Mozzarella made with buffalo milk is the best - it might be hard to find, but it is worth the search.

1. Preheat the oven to 160°C/Gas Mark 3 (325°F).
2. Pierce each tomato with a toothpick to burst the skin. You can cut the tomatoes in half, if you like, or if they are quite large, like the ones in the photo on page 20.
3. Put the tomatoes in a bowl with the basil, garlic, olive oil and a generous pinch of salt and pepper.
4. Mix well with a spoon.
5. Transfer to a baking dish.
6. Roast in the oven for 45 minutes.
7. Carefully remove from the oven.
8. If using the bread, grill under the grill (broiler) or in a griddle (grill) pan over a medium heat until browned. This is your bruschetta.
9. Tear the mozzarella with your hands and put onto four plates.
10. Put a spoonful of tomatoes next to each piece of mozzarella.
11. Drizzle with a little olive oil, and serve with the bruschetta, if you like.

Photo Page 20

PASTA, RISOTTO & GNOCCHI

FUSILLI WITH ZUCCHINI

Ingredients:

2 tablespoons extra-virgin olive oil
500g (1lb 2 oz) zucchini (courgettes),
cut into 1-cm- (½-inch)-thick discs
sea salt and freshly ground black pepper
1 clove garlic, very finely sliced
150g (10 ½ tablespoons) butter (divided)
small bunch basil or parsley, stalks removed
and leaves roughly chopped
320g (11¼ oz) fusilli
50g (¾ cup) freshly grated Parmesan

Serves 4

Equipment:

scale
measuring cups
measuring spoons
sharp knife
grater
2 large saucepans
wooden spoon
colander
cup

This is a regional recipe from the Amalfi coast. The more the zucchini (courgettes) cook down, the creamier they are.

1. Heat the olive oil in a saucepan large enough to hold the courgettes (zucchini) in one layer.
2. Add the courgettes and season well with salt and pepper.
3. Fry over a medium heat for 7–10 minutes until just beginning to brown.
4. Add the garlic and half the butter.
5. Lower the heat.
6. Cook for 10 minutes until the courgettes have become soft and creamy. Add the chopped basil or parsley.
7. Remove from the heat and stir in the remaining butter.
8. Bring a large saucepan of salted water to the boil.
9. Add the fusilli to the pan and cook according to the packet (package) instructions, until cooked but still firm (al dente).
10. Drain, reserving 120 ml (4 fl oz/½ cup) of the cooking water.
11. Stir the cooking water into the courgettes to loosen the sauce.
12. Add the fusilli to the sauce and mix very well with a spoon.
13. Serve with the grated Parmesan.

Photo Page 22

SPAGHETTI ALLE VONGOLE

Ingredients:

4 tablespoons extra-virgin olive oil
4 cloves garlic, finely chopped
3 dried red chillies, crumbled
3kg (6lb 8 oz) small clams, washed thoroughly
bunch of flat-leaf parsley, finely chopped (divided)
sea salt and freshly ground black pepper
400g (14 oz) spaghetti
1 lemon, quartered

Serves 4

Equipment:

scale
measuring cups
measuring spoons
sharp knife
large frying pan
wooden spoon
large saucepan
colander

It is important to toss the spaghetti well with the clams and the juice so they flavour the pasta.

1. Heat the oil in a large frying pan over a medium heat.
2. Add the garlic and fry over a medium heat for 1 minute until just beginning to brown.
3. Add the crumbled chillies, clams and 2 tablespoons of water.
4. Cover and fry over a high heat for about 5 minutes until all the clams open. Discard any that do not open.
5. Add half the parsley to the clams.
6. Season with pepper and some salt if needed; the clams may be salty.
7. Bring a large saucepan of salted water to the boil.
8. Add the spaghetti and cook according to the packet (package) instructions. The spaghetti should be cooked until firm but still with a bite (al dente).
9. Drain the spaghetti and add to the clams.
10. Serve with the remaining parsley and the lemon quarters.

Photo Page 25

PENNE ALL' AMATRICIANA

Ingredients:

2 tablespoons extra-virgin olive oil
250g (9 oz) pancetta or guanciale, cut into fine matchsticks
2 dried red chillies, crumbled
1 red onion, finely chopped
2 tablespoons rosemary leaves
800-g (28-oz) tin plum tomatoes, drained of their juices and crushed
sea salt and freshly ground black pepper
300g (10½ oz) penne
100g (1½ cups) freshly grated pecorino

Equipment:

scale
measuring cups
measuring spoons
tin opener
sharp knife
grater
frying pan
wooden spoon
large saucepan
colander

Serves 4

The secret of a successful amatriciana is the combination of the crisp guanciale or pancetta and the soft onion.

1. **Heat the olive oil in a large frying pan.**
2. **Add the pancetta or guanciale and fry over a medium heat for 8 minutes until it becomes crisp.**
3. **Add the chillies, onion and rosemary to the pan, lower the heat and sweat for 15–20 minutes until the onion becomes transparent.**
4. **Add the tomatoes, season and stir well.**
5. **Bring to the boil, then reduce the heat to low.**
6. **Simmer for 30 minutes until the sauce is very thick.**
7. **Bring a large saucepan of salted water to the boil.**
8. **Cook the penne according to the packet (package) instructions until cooked but still firm (al dente).**
9. **Drain the penne and add to the sauce.**
10. **Mix well and serve with the pecorino.**

Photo Page 27

SPAGHETTI LEMON

Ingredients:

300g (10 ½ oz) spaghetti
juice of 3–4 lemons
150ml (5 fl oz/⅔ cup) extra-virgin olive oil
150g (2 ¼ cups) freshly grated Parmesan
sea salt and freshly ground black pepper
2 handfuls basil,
leaves picked and chopped
grated zest of 1 lemon

Serves 4

Equipment:

scale
measuring cups
measuring spoons
grater
sharp knife
large saucepan
bowl
whisk
spoon
colander

This is the freshest tasting pasta you can cook. The lemon makes it zesty and summery. Roll the lemons on a work counter before cutting them to release the juice.

1. Bring a large saucepan of salted water to the boil.
2. Cook the spaghetti according to the packet (package) instructions until cooked but still firm (al dente).
3. Meanwhile, in a bowl, whisk the lemon juice with the olive oil.
4. Stir in the Parmesan; as it melts in, the mixture will become thick and creamy.
5. Season with salt and pepper.
6. Drain the spaghetti and return to the pan.
7. Add the sauce to the spaghetti, and shake the pan so that each strand of pasta is coated with the cheese mixture.
8. Stir in the chopped basil and the lemon zest.

Photo Page 28

RISOTTO WITH TOMATO AND BASIL

Ingredients:

600g (1lb 5 oz) tomatoes
3 tablespoons extra-virgin olive oil
100g (7 tablespoons) butter (divided)
1 red onion, finely chopped
3 cloves garlic, chopped
1 celery heart, finely chopped
300g (1½ cups) carnaroli rice or
other risotto rice
small bunch of basil, leaves picked
sea salt
1.2 litres (40 fl oz/5 cups) hot
chicken stock (broth) see page 162
100g (1 cup) freshly grated Parmesan,
plus extra for sprinkling

Serves 6

Equipment:

scale
measuring cups
measuring spoons
sharp knife
slotted spoon
grater
large bowl
large saucepan
paring knife
frying pan
wooden spoon
ladle

This is a great risotto to make in the summer when the tomatoes are ripe and the basil is fresh and full of flavour.

1. Fill a large bowl with ice water.
2. Bring a large saucepan of water to the boil.
3. Using a paring knife, carefully score an x into the skin of each tomato.
4. Carefully put the scored tomatoes in the boiling water, boil for 1 minute and carefully remove them from the boiling water with a slotted spoon and put in the ice water.
5. When cool, peel the tomatoes with your fingers; the skin should come away easily and then tear the flesh into rough pieces.
6. Heat the olive oil and half the butter in a heavy frying pan.
7. Add the onion, garlic and celery and gently fry, stirring, for 10 minutes until soft.
8. Add the rice, stirring well, to mix with the vegetables.
9. Fry the rice for 5 minutes. Add the tomatoes, tear the basil and add to the pan. Season with salt.
10. Cook for 3–4 minutes, stirring constantly, until the liquid from the tomatoes has evaporated.
11. Add a ladleful of the stock. When the rice has absorbed most of the stock, add another ladleful.
12. Continue adding two ladles at a time, only adding more when the preceeding ladlefuls have been absorbed.
13. Cook, stirring constantly, for 15 minutes until the rice is cooked but firm.
14. Stir in the remaining butter and the Parmesan.
15. Serve with more Parmesan on top.

Photo Page 30

CASARECCE WITH PESTO

Ingredients:

200g (1½ cups) basil leaves
200g (3 cups) freshly grated Parmesan
½ clove garlic
75g (⅔ cup) pine nuts
200ml (7 fl oz/scant 1 cup) extra-virgin olive oil
sea salt and freshly ground black pepper
450g (1lb) casarecce pasta

Serves 6

Equipment:

scale
measuring cups
grater
food processor
large saucepan
colander
wooden spoon

Making pesto in a food processor makes it pale, smooth and creamy. In Liguria fine green beans and potato pieces are often added to the pasta.

1. Put the basil leaves, Parmesan, garlic and pine nuts into a food processor fitted with a sharp blade.
2. Add the olive oil and some salt and pepper.
3. Blitz together to make a smooth paste.
4. Bring a large saucepan of salted water to the boil.
5. Add the casarecce to the pan and cook according to the packet (package) instructions, until firm (al dente).
6. Drain, then return to the pan. Add the pesto and mix well.

Photo Page 33

CACIO E PEPE

Ingredients:

sea salt
300g (10 ½ oz) spaghetti
½ tablespoon freshly ground black pepper
150g (10 ½ tablespoons) butter
250g (1 ½ cups) freshly grated pecorino (divided)

Serves 4

Equipment:

measuring cups
measuring spoons
grater
large saucepan
cup
colander
frying pan
wooden spoon

The pepper turns this simple dish into something special. You must always add the pasta to the sauce and it is important to stir this well so that it becomes rich and creamy.

1. Bring a large saucepan of salted water to the boil.
2. Add the spaghetti to the pan and cook according to the packet (package) instructions until firm (al dente).
3. Drain the spaghetti, reserving 120 ml (4 fl oz/½ cup) of the cooking water.
4. Heat a frying pan over a medium heat.
5. Add the pasta water, pepper and butter.
6. Mix well with a wooden spoon.
7. Remove from the heat.
8. Stir in half the pecorino.
9. Add the spaghetti and mix with the spoon to coat well.
10. Serve with the remaining cheese.

Photo Page 35

RIGATONI WITH PORK RAGU

Ingredients:

3 tablespoons extra-virgin olive oil
100g (3½ oz) pancetta,
cut into thin matchsticks
25g (2 tablespoons) butter
1 red onion, finely chopped
1 small leek, finely chopped
1 celery heart, finely chopped
2 cloves garlic, finely chopped
½ teaspoon chopped thyme leaves
sea salt and freshly ground black pepper
500g (1lb 2 oz) minced (ground) pork
1 teaspoon chopped sage
300ml (10 fl oz/1¼ cups) chicken
stock (broth) see page 162
150ml (5 fl oz/⅔ cup) milk
peel of ½ lemon
450g (1 lb) rigatoni

Serves 4–5

Equipment:

scale
measuring cups
measuring spoons
largy heavy frying pan
wooden spoon

The finer you can cut the celery, onion, leek and garlic the better.

1. Heat the olive oil in a large heavy frying pan over a medium heat.
2. Add the pancetta and fry for 5 minutes.
3. Add the butter, onion, leek, celery, garlic, thyme and season with salt and pepper.
4. Fry, stirring regularly with a wooden spoon, for about 15 minutes.
5. Add the pork and sage.
6. Fry for 5 minutes until the pork is no longer pink.
7. Stir in the stock (broth), milk and lemon peel.
8. Bring to the boil.
9. Reduce the heat to a simmer.
10. Simmer for 1 hour until most of the liquid has evaporated. Top up with water if necessary.
11. Meanwhile, bring a large saucepan of salted water to the boil.
12. Add the rigatoni to the pan and according to the packet (package) instructions until film (al dente).
13. Drain and add the pasta to the sauce.
14. Stir well and serve.

Photo Page 36

SPAGHETTI WITH PEAS AND PROSCIUTTO

Ingredients:

100g (7 tablespoons) butter
150g (5½ oz) spring onions (scallions), sliced
375g (2½ cups) peas
sea salt and freshly ground black pepper
3 tablespoons hot water
1 clove garlic , thinly sliced
2 tablespoons chopped flat-leaf parsley
3 tablespoons extra-virgin olive oil
150g (5½ oz) prosciutto slices, torn into small pieces
300g (10½ oz) spaghetti
50g (¾ cup) freshly grated Parmesan

Serves 4

Equipment:

scale
measuring cups
measuring spoons
sharp knife
grater
frying pan
wooden spoon
large saucepan
colander
cup

In the summer, you can use basil instead of parsley.

1. Heat the butter in a heavy frying pan over a medium heat.
2. Add the spring onions (scallions) and fry, stirring for 4 minutes until soft.
3. Add the peas, a good pinch of salt and pepper and 3 tablespoons of hot water.
4. Reduce heat to low and cook for 5 minutes, or until the water has evaporated.
5. Add the garlic, parsley and the olive oil.
6. Cover and cook over a low heat for 15 minutes.
7. Add the prosciutto and cook for 5 minutes.
8. Bring a large saucepan of salted water to the boil.
9. Add the spaghetti and cook according to the packet (package) instructions until firm (al dente).
10. Drain, keeping a splash of the cooking water.
11. Add the spaghetti to the pea mixture.
12. Stir well with the spoon.
13. Stir in the pasta water.
14. Top with the Parmesan and serve immediately.

Photo Page 39

SPAGHETTI CARBONARA

Ingredients:

1 tablespoon extra-virgin olive oil
150g (5½ oz) sliced pancetta,
cut into thin matchsticks
sea salt and freshly ground black pepper
1 red onion, finely chopped
200g (2¼ cups) freshly grated Parmesan,
plus extra to serve
4 medium (large) egg yolks
300g (10½ oz) spaghetti

Serves 4

Equipment:

scale
measuring cups
sharp knife
grater
large frying pan
wooden spoon
bowl
fork
large saucepan
colander
cup

Warm the eggs and Parmesan by adding a spoonful of water from the pasta pot as this will stop them from scrambling.

1. Heat the olive oil in a large frying pan over a medium heat.
2. Add the pancetta with a pinch of black pepper.
3. Fry over a medium heat for 5 minutes.
4. Add the onion and fry for 5 minutes until it is golden.
5. Remove the pan from the heat.
6. In a bowl, use a fork to mix the Parmesan with the egg yolks.
7. Bring a large saucepan of salted water to the boil.
8. Add the spaghetti and cook according to the packet (package) instructions until firm (al dente).
9. Drain, reserving 250ml (8 fl oz/1 cup) of the cooking water.
10. With the pan still off the heat, mix the hot spaghetti in with the pancetta and onion mixture using a wooden spoon.
11. Stir in the egg mixture and the reserved pasta water.
12. Mix well until it forms a creamy sauce.
13. Serve immediately with extra grated Parmesan on top.

Photo Page 41

PENNE WITH QUICK SAUSAGE SAUCE

Ingredients:

125ml (4¼ fl oz/generous ½ cup) extra-virgin olive oil
2 red onions, chopped
2 cloves garlic, chopped
5 Italian spiced pork sausages, skinned and meat crumbled
2 bay leaves
1½ tablespoons chopped rosemary
1 teaspoon dried chilli (red pepper) flakes
sea salt and freshly ground black pepper
800g (28 oz) tin peeled plum tomatoes, mashed with a fork
250g (3 cups) penne
100ml (3½ fl oz/scant ½ cup) double (heavy) cream
120g (scant 2 cups) freshly grated Parmesan

Serves 4

Equipment:

scale
measuring cups
measuring spoons
tin opener
fork
grater
large frying pan
wooden spoon
large saucepan
colander
cup

Sometimes you need a fast and reliable pasta recipe and this is one we love. Make sure you crumble the sausages finely before you cook them.

1. Heat the olive oil in a large frying pan over a medium heat.
2. Add the onions and garlic and fry for 8 minutes until light brown.
3. Add the crumbled sausages, bay leaves, rosemary, chilli (red pepper) flakes and salt and pepper.
4. Increase the heat to high and cook for 20 minutes, stirring with a wooden spoon to mash the sausages, until the sausage meat is brown.
5. Stir in the tomatoes and bring to the boil.
6. Reduce the heat to low and simmer for 15 minutes.
7. Remove the pan from the heat.
8. Bring a large saucepan of salted water to the boil.
9. Add the penne to the pan and cook according to the packet (package) instructions until firm (al dente).
10. Drain the penne, reserving 120 ml (4 fl oz/½ cup) of the cooking water.
11. Stir the cream into the tomato sauce along with the drained penne, the reserved pasta water and half the Parmesan.
12. Mix well and serve with the remaining Parmesan.

Photo Page 42

GNOCCHI WITH TOMATO SAUCE

Ingredients:

2 tablespoons **extra-virgin olive oil**
3 **red onions**, finely sliced
2 cloves **garlic**, finely sliced
800g (28 oz) tin peeled **plum tomatoes**
sea salt and freshly ground **black pepper**
1kg (2lb 4 oz) white
floury potatoes, washed
130g (1 cup) **00 flour**
1 large (extra-large) **egg**,
lightly beaten
10 **basil** leaves

Serves 6

Equipment:

scale
measuring cups
sharp knife
tin opener
small bowl
fork
large frying pan
wooden spoon
large saucepan
colander
blunt knife
Mouli grater (food mill) or
potato ricer
sieve
slotted spoon

Gnocchi should be made as light as possible. A potato ricer gets great results. If you're using tomatoes with a lot of juice, put them in a colander to drain them.

1. Heat the olive oil in a large frying pan over a medium heat.
2. Add the onions and garlic and fry for 10 minutes until soft.
3. Add the tomatoes and stir to break them up.
4. Season with salt and pepper.
5. Cook over the lowest heat while you make the gnocchi.
6. Bring a large saucepan of salted water to the boil and add potatoes.
7. Cook for 20–25 minutes until they are easily pierced with a fork. Drain.
8. When potatoes are cool enough to handle, peel them with a blunt knife.
9. Immediately put the potatoes through a Mouli grater (food mill) or potato ricer onto a clean work counter.
10. Sift the flour over the warm potatoes and make a well in the centre.
11. Add the beaten egg.
12. Using your hands, quickly mix to form a smooth, soft dough. Do not overwork the dough or you will make the gnocchi too chewy.
13. Divide the dough into four.
14. Using your hands, roll the dough into a sausage of 1.5cm (⅝ inch) diameter.
15. Cut these into 2.5cm (1-inch)-long pieces with a knife.
16. Bring a large saucepan of salted water to the boil and cook the gnocchi for 3 minutes until they rise to the surface. Remove with a slotted spoon.
17. Remove the tomato sauce from the heat and stir in the basil.
18. Put the gnocchi into the pan, mix well and serve.

Photo Page 45

SOUP

PUMPKIN SOUP

Ingredients:

3 tablespoons **extra-virgin olive oil**, plus extra to serve
50g (3½ tablespoons) **butter**
2 cloves **garlic**, very finely sliced
1 tablespoon **sage** leaves
1.5kg (3lb 5 oz) **pumpkin**, peeled, deseeded (seeded) and cut into large cubes
1 large **potato**, peeled and cubed
1 **red chilli**
sea salt and freshly ground **black pepper**
1 litre (34 fl oz/4¼ cups) **chicken stock** (**broth**) see page 162
3 tablespoons freshly grated **Parmesan**, to serve
1 tablespoon **crème fraîche**, to serve

Serves 6

Equipment:

scale
measuring cups
measuring spoons
sharp knife
wooden spoon
large saucepan
strainer
food processor

This is a great dish to make in the autumn when pumpkins are at their best. Cutting pumpkin can be very difficult so make sure you have someone to help you.

1. Heat the olive oil and butter in a pan over a medium heat.
2. Add the garlic and sage leaves and fry for 5 minutes.
3. Add the pumpkin and potato, then fry for 1 minute.
4. Add the chilli and season well with salt and pepper.
5. Pour in enough stock to just cover the pumpkin.
6. Bring to the boil.
7. Reduce the heat to low and simmer for 20–25 minutes until the pumpkin is tender.
8. Strain about one third of the stock (broth) from the pumpkin into a bowl and set aside.
9. Pour what is left in the pan into a food processor.
10. Pulse quickly until the mixture is very thick.
11. Return the mixture to the pan.
12. Add the strained stock and stir. The soup will be very thick.
13. Taste, then add more salt and pepper, if needed.
14. Serve with the Parmesan, a drizzle of olive oil and the crème fraîche on top.

Photo Page 46

PAPPA AL POMODORO

Ingredients:

4kg (8lb 12 oz) ripe plum tomatoes
5 tablespoons extra-virgin olive oil (divided)
2 cloves garlic, sliced
sea salt and freshly ground black pepper
1 stale sourdough loaf, crust removed
large bunch of basil, leaves torn

Serves 8

Equipment:

scale
measuring cups
measuring spoons
sharp knife
large bowl
large saucepan
paring knife
slotted spoon
frying pan
wooden spoon

If the bread is stale it absorbs and cooks better. If you only have fresh bread, toast it in the oven to dry it out first.

1. Fill a large bowl with ice water.
2. Bring a large saucepan of water to the boil.
3. Using a paring knife, carefully score an x into the skin of each tomato.
4. Carefully put the scored tomatoes in the boiling water and boil for 1 minute.
5. Remove with a slotted spoon and immediately put in the ice water.
6. When cool enough to handle, peel the tomatoes with your fingers; the skin should come away easily from the scored area.
7. Halve the tomatoes and squeeze out the seeds and juice.
8. Roughly chop the tomatoes.
9. Heat 3 tablespoons of the olive oil in a frying pan over a medium heat.
10. Add the garlic and fry for 4 minutes.
11. Add the tomatoes.
12. Simmer, stirring occasionally, for 30 minutes until the sauce is thick.
13. Season well with salt and pepper.
14. Add 600ml (20 fl oz/2½ cups) water.
15. Bring to the boil.
16. Add the bread and stir until it absorbs the liquid.
17. Remove the pan from the heat.
18. Allow to cool slightly, adding more water if it is too thick.
19. Stir the basil and the remaining 2 tablespoons of olive oil into the soup.
20. Serve at room temperature.

Photo Page 48

CHICKEN STOCK

Ingredients:

1 × 1.5–2kg (3lb 5 oz–4lb 8 oz) organic
boiling fowl (boiling hen) or large chicken
1 small red onion
2 large onions
1 celery heart
2 tomatoes
1 head garlic
bunch of parsley
3 sprigs thyme
5 bay leaves
1 teaspoon black peppercorns
sea salt and freshly ground black pepper

Serves 6–8

Equipment:

scale
measuring cups
measuring spoons
large saucepan
slotted spoons
small sieve
strainer
large bowl

There are a few essential recipes to learn and chicken stock is one of them. We like to make ours very light. You can easily make it into a soup by adding tiny pasta shapes and topping it with Parmesan as on page 51.

1. Put all the ingredients, apart from the salt, into a large saucepan with 3 litres (3 quarts) cold water.
2. Bring to the boil.
3. Reduce the heat.
4. Skim the fat and any bits that have risen to the surface with a small sieve or skimmer.
5. Gently simmer for 1 hour.
6. Carefully remove the chicken from the pot with some slotted spoons.
7. Pour the stock into a strainer over a very large bowl to strain out the vegetables and herbs.
8. Season the stock (broth) with salt and pepper.

Photo Page 51

VEGETABLES

SMASHED POTATOES WITH GREEN BEANS

Ingredients:

1.3kg (3 lb) waxy potatoes such as Charlotte or Fingerling, peeled
sea salt and freshly ground black pepper
200g (7 oz) fine green beans
100g (1½ cups) freshly grated Parmesan
75–100ml (2½–3½ fl oz/⅓–½ cup) extra-virgin olive oil

Serves 4

Equipment:

scale
measuring cups
vegetable peeler
grater
2 large saucepans
colander
large bowl
fork

Cook the green beans well, not al dente, so they combine nicely with the potatoes.

1. Put the potatoes in a large saucepan, then cover with salted water and bring to the boil.
2. Reduce the heat and simmer for 25–30 minutes until the potatoes are easily pierced with a fork.
3. Bring another pan of salted water to the boil.
4. Add the green beans to the pan, boil for 5 minutes and then drain and set aside.
5. Drain the potatoes, then put them in a large bowl.
6. Mash using a fork or potato masher until there are no lumps.
7. Add the green beans to the potatoes and mix well.
8. Add the Parmesan, olive oil and a pinch of black pepper and mix in with the fork.

Photo Page 53

LENTILS

Ingredients:

250g (generous 1 cup) brown lentils
2–3 cloves garlic
small bunch of sage
1 chilli (optional)
3 tablespoons extra-virgin olive oil
sea salt and freshly ground black pepper

Serves 4

Equipment:

scale
measuring cups
measuring spoons
heavy saucepan
sieve
wooden spoon

It is important to taste the lentils to see when they are done. You can also add fresh, chopped herbs to serve.

1. Put the lentils, garlic, sage and chilli, if using, in a heavy saucepan and cover with cold water.
2. Bring to the boil.
3. Reduce the heat and simmer for 15–20 minutes until tender. Add more water during cooking if it all gets absorbed by the lentils before they are done.
4. Drain the lentils in a sieve.
5. Return the lentils to the pan.
6. Stir in the olive oil and add salt and pepper to taste.

Photo Page 55

ZUCCHINI SALAD

Ingredients:

1kg (2lb 4 oz) courgettes (zucchini), ends trimmed
sea salt and freshly ground black pepper
2 tablespoons extra-virgin olive oil
juice of 1 lemon
10 basil leaves
100g (3 ½ oz) washed rocket (arugula) leaves
100g (3 ½ oz) Parmesan

Serves 8

Equipment:

scale
measuring spoons
sharp knife
lemon squeezer
potato peeler
large bowl

When choosing a courgette (zucchini), look for the freshest small ones. Soak them in cold water for 30 minutes before peeling them into ribbons, to firm them up.

1. Using a potato peeler, peel the courgettes into ribbons into a large bowl.
2. Season the ribbons with salt and pepper.
3. Add the olive oil and the lemon juice.
4. Add the basil and rocket (arugula).
5. Using the potato peeler, shave over the Parmesan.

Photo Page 56

ZUCCHINI TRIFOLATI

Ingredients:

750g (1lb 10 oz) courgettes (zucchini), ends trimmed
3 tablespoons extra-virgin olive oil
2 cloves garlic, finely sliced
2 tablespoons chopped mint leaves
2 tablespoons chopped basil leaves
4 tablespoons hot water
sea salt and freshly ground black pepper

Serves 6

Equipment:

scale
measuring spoons
sharp knife
large frying pan
wooden spoon

You can make this dish with different coloured courgettes (zucchini). It is also delicious at room temperature.

1. Carefully cut the courgettes (zucchini) at an angle into 1.5-cm (⅝-inch) wedges.
2. Heat olive oil in a large heavy frying pan over a medium-high heat.
3. Carefully add the courgettes. Cook for 5 minutes until slightly browned.
4. Using a spoon, turn the courgettes over and cook for another 5 minutes.
5. Add the garlic and 1 tablespoon each of mint and basil. Stir to combine.
6. Reduce the heat to low and cook for 10 minutes.
7. Add 4 tablespoons of hot water. Cook until the water is absorbed and the courgettes are soft.
8. Stir in the remaining 1 tablespoon each of mint and basil.
9. Season to taste with salt and pepper.
10. Transfer to a serving platter. Serve.

Photo Page 58

SLOW-ROASTED TOMATOES WITH BASIL

Ingredients:

12 ripe plum tomatoes,
halved lengthways
sea salt and freshly ground black pepper
6 tablespoons extra-virgin olive oil
2 cloves garlic, very finely sliced
24 basil leaves

Serves 6

Equipment:

scale
measuring spoons
baking sheet
wooden spoon
oven gloves

Cooking this on a very low heat dries out the tomatoes, concentrates the flavour and makes them sweeter.

1. Preheat the oven to 110°C/Gas Mark ¼ (225°F) or the lowest temperature.
2. Put the tomatoes on a baking sheet, side by side.
3. Season well with salt and pepper and drizzle with half the olive oil.
4. Top each tomato with a thin piece of garlic and a basil leaf.
5. Roast in the oven for 2 hours 30 minutes. Every 30 minutes, gently flatten the tomatoes with a spoon, releasing their juices and concentrating the flavour.
6. Carefully remove from the oven and serve at room temperature, drizzled with the remaining olive oil.

Photo Page 60

SLOW-COOKED PEAS

Ingredients:

100g (7 tablespoons) butter
250g (9 oz) spring onions (scallions), roughly chopped
750g (4 ⅔ cups) podded (shelled) peas
5 cloves garlic, sliced
3 tablespoons chopped flat-leaf parsley
4 tablespoons hot water
sea salt and freshly ground black pepper
2 tablespoons extra-virgin olive oil

Serves 6

Equipment:

scale
measuring cups
measuring spoons
sharp knife
heavy frying pan
wooden spoon

If you can find them, buy peas in their pod and pod them yourself. You may find pre-podded peas need a little more water.

1. Gently melt the butter in a heavy frying pan.
2. Add the spring onions (scallions) and fry over a medium heat until they soften and begin to brown.
3. Add the peas and garlic and fry for 2–3 minutes.
4. Stir in the parsley and 4 tablespoons of hot water.
5. Season well with salt and pepper.
6. Cover the pan with a lid and simmer for 15 minutes. If the peas dry up, add some more water.
7. Remove from the heat and add the olive oil.

Photo Page 62

GREEN BEANS IN TOMATO

Ingredients:

500g (1lb 2 oz) ripe plum tomatoes (or other fleshy variety)
2 tablespoons extra-virgin olive oil, plus extra for drizzling
2 cloves garlic, finely sliced
sea salt and freshly ground black pepper
750g (7 ½ cups) green beans, top stem removed
20 basil leaves

Serves 6

Equipment:

scale
measuring cups
measuring spoons
large bowl
large saucepan
paring knife
slotted spoon
heavy frying pan
wooden spoon
colander

We like to make this in the summer when the beans and tomatoes are in season.

1. Fill a large bowl with ice water.
2. Bring a large saucepan of water to the boil.
3. Using a paring knife, carefully score an x into the skin of each tomato.
4. Carefully put the scored tomatoes in the boiling water and boil for 1 minute.
5. Remove with a slotted spoon and immediately put in the ice water.
6. When cool enough to handle, peel the tomatoes with your fingers; the skin should come away easily from the scored area.
7. Halve the tomatoes and squeeze out the seeds and juice.
8. Roughly chop the tomatoes.
9. Heat the olive oil in a heavy frying pan over a medium heat.
10. Add the garlic, then fry for 2 minutes, or until soft.
11. Add the tomatoes and season well with salt and pepper.
12. Cook for about 10 minutes until the tomatoes thicken into a sauce.
13. Bring a large saucepan of salted water to the boil.
14. Add the beans to the pan and boil for 5 minutes until soft.
15. Drain the beans.
16. Add the beans to the tomato sauce and stir to mix.
17. Cook for 10 minutes.
18. Season with salt and pepper and stir in the basil.
19. Serve drizzled with olive oil.

Photo Page 65

ROASTED VEGETABLES

Ingredients:

2 fennel bulbs, outer leaves removed
250g (9 oz) butternut squash,
peeled, deseeded (seeded) and cut
into 3-cm (1¼-inch) pieces
6 carrots, cut at an angle into
3-cm (1¼-inch)-thick slices
4 cloves garlic, halved
sea salt and freshly ground black pepper
4 tablespoons extra-virgin olive oil

Serves 6

Equipment:

scale
measuring spoons
sharp knife
vegetable peeler
large saucepan
colander
large bowl
wooden spoon
baking sheet
tongs

This is an autumnal selection. Roasting vegetables brings out their natural sweetness. In the summer you might like to try aubergines (eggplants), tomatoes and courgettes (zucchini).

1. Preheat the oven to 200°C/Gas Mark 6 (400°F).
2. Bring a saucepan of salted water to the boil over a high heat.
3. Cut each fennel bulb in half. Cut each half into 3 wedges.
4. Carefully lower the fennel into the water.
5. Cook for 3 minutes.
6. Drain using a colander.
7. Transfer to a large bowl.
8. Add the squash, carrots and garlic.
9. Season with salt and pepper and add the olive oil. Mix together to evenly coat the vegetables.
10. Transfer the vegetables to a baking sheet and carefully put into the oven.
11. Roast for 30 minutes.
12. Using tongs, turn the pieces over.
13. Roast for another 15 minutes, or until the vegetables are soft.
14. Carefully remove from the oven and serve.

Photo Page 66

ROASTED RED AND YELLOW PEPPERS

Ingredients:

3 red (bell) peppers
3 yellow (bell) peppers
1 clove garlic, very finely sliced
1 teaspoon dried wild oregano
1 tablespoon fresh oregano
3 tablespoons olive oil
sea salt and freshly ground black pepper

Serves 6

Equipment:

sharp knife
measuring spoons
small bowl
spoon
pastry brush
baking sheet
oven gloves

The most important thing is to make sure there is not one single seed in the peppers before they go in the oven. Don't be afraid to roast them too long because they get better the longer they cook.

1. **Preheat the oven to 200°C/Gas Mark 6 (400°F).**
2. **Cut the peppers in half lengthways and then each piece again, into three, at an angle.**
3. **Remove the seeds and white pith.**
4. **In a small bowl, combine the garlic, both oreganos and olive oil and mix well.**
5. **Season the peppers and brush with the mixture.**
6. **Place the peppers, skin side down, on a baking sheet and bake for 30 minutes, or until the edges are slightly browned and the flesh is completely soft.**
7. **Remove from the oven.**

Photo Page 68

ROASTED DATTERINI TOMATOES

Ingredients:

750g (1lb 2 oz) red and yellow datterini tomatoes
2 cloves garlic
2 tablespoons olive oil
10 sprigs thyme
sea salt and freshly ground black pepper

Serves 4

Equipment:

scale
measuring spoons
toothpick
bowl
baking sheet
oven gloves

These tomatoes are best eaten at room temperature. If you can't find both colours, just use one.

1. Preheat the oven to 150°C/Gas Mark 2 (300°F)
2. Wash the tomatoes and prick them with a toothpick.
3. Put them in a bowl with the olive oil, garlic and thyme.
4. Season with salt and pepper.
5. Spread out on a baking sheet without overcrowding.
6. Roast for 1–1½ hours, drain any juice halfway through. They should be concentrated.
7. Carefully remove from the oven.

Photo Page 70

TUSCAN ROASTED POTATOES

Ingredients:

10 cloves garlic
1.5kg (3lb 5 oz) potatoes,
peeled and cut into 2-cm (¾-inch) cubes
bunch of rosemary, leaves picked
sea salt and freshly ground black pepper
200ml (7 fl oz/scant 1 cup) extra-virgin olive oil

Serves 8

Equipment:

scale
measuring cups
blunt knife
ceramic roasting tray (pan)
oven gloves

Try to use a waxy potato rather than a floury one for this recipe.

1. Preheat the oven to 180°C/Gas Mark 4 (350°F).
2. Carefully squash the garlic cloves with the flat of a knife.
3. Put the potatoes, garlic and rosemary into a ceramic roasting tray (pan) large enough to hold them in one layer.
4. Add a large pinch of salt and pepper, then pour the olive oil over and mix with your hands.
5. Roast in the oven for 1 hour, stirring or shaking the tray from time to time, until golden brown.
6. Carefully remove the potatoes from the oven.

Photo Page 73

ROASTED POTATOES WITH LEMON AND THYME

Ingredients:

2 thick-skinned lemons,
stalks and tips removed
750g (1lb 10 oz) potatoes,
quartered lengthways
4 cloves garlic, halved lengthways
3 tablespoons thyme leaves
sea salt and freshly ground black pepper
4 tablespoons extra-virgin olive oil

Serves 6

Equipment:

scale
measuring spoons
sharp knife
large bowl
spoon
ovenproof dish
oven gloves

Lemon and potatoes are an unusual combination that works especially well with chicken and fish.

1. Preheat the oven to 220°C/Gas Mark 7 (425°F).
2. Halve the lemons lengthways, then cut each half into three lengthways, then halve each piece widthways, so you have 24 pieces of lemon.
3. Put the potatoes and lemon pieces in a bowl.
4. Mix, squeezing the juice out of the lemons with your hands.
5. Add the garlic and thyme, season well with salt and pepper, then add the olive oil and mix well.
6. Put the potatoes in an ovenproof dish.
7. Roast in the oven for 40 minutes, turning halfway through until golden brown.
8. Carefully remove from the oven.

Photo Page 75

STUFFED SQUASH

Ingredients:

2 small onion squash (red kuri)
sea salt and freshly ground black pepper
1 teaspoon dried chilli (red pepper) flakes
120ml (4 fl oz/½ cup) extra-virgin olive oil
500g (1lb 2 oz) potatoes,
cut into 2 cm (¾-inch) cubes
150g (5½ oz) pancetta,
finely sliced into matchsticks
2 tablespoons thyme leaves
3 cloves garlic, finely chopped

Serves 6

Equipment:

scale
measuring cups
measuring spoons
sharp knife
baking sheet
large saucepan
colander
bowl
wooden spoon
oven gloves
fork

This is dramatic and celebratory. If the squash appears to be browning too quickly on the edges and uncooked in the centre, just splash a little water over it and cover it with aluminium foil as it finishes cooking.

1. **Preheat the oven to 220°C/Gas Mark 7 (425°F).**
2. **Carefully cut off the top quarter of each squash with a knife.**
3. **Scoop out the seeds with a spoon.**
4. **Season the insides with salt, pepper and chilli.**
5. **Put the squash onto the baking sheet.**
6. **Drizzle half the olive oil generously over the squash, both inside and out.**
7. **Roast the squash in the oven for 15 minutes.**
8. **Meanwhile, bring a large saucepan of salted water to the boil.**
9. **Add the potatoes to the pan and boil for 8 minutes.**
10. **Drain the potatoes.**
11. **Put the potatoes, pancetta, thyme and garlic in a bowl and season with salt and pepper and stir to combine.**
12. **Drizzle with the remaining olive oil.**
13. **Remove the squash from the oven.**
14. **Spoon the potato mixture into the squash.**
15. **Return to the oven to bake for another 30–40 minutes.**
16. **Test for doneness by sticking a fork into the side of each squash: the flesh should be soft and almost falling apart.**
17. **Carefully remove from the oven.**

Photo Page 77

FISH

SEA BASS OVER POTATOES

Ingredients:

250g (1⅔ cups) cherry tomatoes
500g (1 lb 2 oz) potatoes, peeled
2 tablespoons extra-virgin olive oil,
plus extra for greasing
4 bay leaves
sea salt and freshly ground black pepper
4 sea bass fillets
juice of 1 large lemon

Serves 4

Equipment:

scale
measuring cups
measuring spoons
vegetable peeler
sharp knife
large saucepan
colander
roasting tray (pan)

If you slice the potatoes after they have been boiled, they will keep their shape better.

1. Preheat the oven to 200°C/Gas Mark 6 (400°F).
2. Halve the tomatoes and squeeze out the seeds and juice.
3. Bring a large saucepan of salted water to the boil.
4. Add the potatoes to the pan and boil for 10 minutes until cooked but still firm.
5. Drain the potatoes and leave to cool.
6. Slice the cooked potatoes lengthways.
7. Drizzle a roasting tray (pan) with 2 tablespoons of olive oil.
8. Cover the tray with the sliced potatoes and tomato halves, put the bay leaves on top and season well with salt and pepper.
9. Put the bass fillets on top and drizzle with olive oil.
10. Roast in the oven for 6 minutes.
11. Remove from the oven, then squeeze over the lemon juice.
12. Return to the oven and roast for another 6 minutes.
13. Carefully remove from the oven and serve each portion spooned over with juices from the pan.

Photo Page 78

SPIEDINI OF MONKFISH AND SCALLOPS

Ingredients:

6 (15cm/6 inch) sprigs rosemary
500g (1lb 2 oz) monkfish tail,
deboned (boned) and skinned
12 medium scallops
sea salt and freshly ground black pepper
extra-virgin olive oil, for brushing
2 lemons, cut into wedges, to serve

Serves 6

Equipment:

scale
sharp knife
pastry brush
chargrill (char broiler) or griddle (grill) pan

Cooking the fish on a rosemary skewer gently flavours the fish. Choose the longest rosemary branches you can find.

1. Pull most of the leaves off the rosemary sprigs, leaving just the tufts at the end.
2. Cut the monkfish into twelve cubes roughly the same size as the scallops.
3. For each rosemary sprig, you need two scallops and two cubes of monkfish.
4. Thread a rosemary sprig through a scallop.
5. Next, thread through a piece of monkfish, then another scallop and then another piece of monkfish.
6. Repeat for the remaining rosemary sprigs.
7. Season the spiedini on all sides with salt and pepper, then brush with olive oil to prevent them sticking to the grill.
8. Warm a chargrill (char broiler) or griddle (grill) pan over a high heat.
9. Grill the spiedini for 3 minutes, or until the spiedini no longer stick but have sealed and turned brown.
10. Turn the spiedini and grill for another 3 minutes. The fish should be white and cooked through.
11. Serve with the lemon wedges.

Photo Page 81

MONKFISH WRAPPED IN PANCETTA

Ingredients:

4 (160g/5¾-oz) portions monkfish tail, deboned (boned) and skinned
sea salt and freshly ground black pepper
16 thin slices pancetta
1 sprig rosemary, leaves picked
3 tablespoons extra-virgin olive oil
2 lemons, cut into wedges

Serves 4

Equipment:

scale
measuring spoons
sharp knife
large ovenproof frying pan
tongs
oven gloves

Don't wrap the parcels too tightly. Before you put the parcels in the oven, it is important to sear them in a hot pan so that they don't stick.

1. Preheat the oven to 200°C/Gas Mark 6 (400°F).
2. Season the monkfish portions with salt and pepper.
3. On a sheet of baking (parchment) paper, lay four pieces of pancetta, slightly overlapping, to create a rectangle that will cover the monkfish portion.
4. Lay the monkfish portion on top of the pancetta and use the baking paper to wrap the pancetta around the fish. Remove the paper.
5. Tuck a few rosemary leaves into the pancetta.
6. Repeat for the other three pieces of monkfish.
7. Heat the olive oil in a large ovenproof frying pan.
8. Add the wrapped monkfish, seam side up.
9. Sear for 1 minute over a high heat, then turn over with tongs.
10. Put the pan in the oven and roast for 10 minutes.
11. When cooked, the flesh of the fish should be white thoughout.
12. Carefully remove from the oven and serve each portion with juices from the pan spooned over.

Photo Page 83

MEAT

SPATCHCOCK CHICKEN IN MILK

Ingredients:

1 large (1.5kg/3lb 5 oz) organic chicken,
boneless spatchcocked (ask your butcher to do this)
sea salt and freshly ground black pepper
80g (5½ tablespoons) butter
500ml (17 fl oz/generous 2 cups) milk
1 lemon, halved
2 cloves garlic
10 sage leaves

Serves 6

Equipment:

scale
measuring cups
measuring spoons
heavy ovenproof frying pan
wooden spoon
tongs
skewer
oven gloves

A spatchcock (or butterflied) chicken, is chicken with the backbone removed, which allows for quicker and even cooking. It can be a bit tricky to do, so we recommend asking the butcher to do it for you.

1. Preheat the oven to 220°C/Gas Mark 7 (425°F).
2. Season the chicken on both sides with salt and pepper.
3. Melt the butter in a heavy ovenproof frying pan, large enough to hold the chicken, over a medium-high heat.
4. Add the chicken, skin side down, to the pan and cook for 7 minutes until the skin is golden.
5. Cover with the milk and squeeze over the lemon.
6. Add the garlic and sage to the pan, then fry for 1 minute.
7. Carefully flip the chicken over with tongs.
8. Put the pan in the oven and cook for 15 minutes.
9. To test for doneness, pierce the thickest part of the thigh; the juices should run clear. The milk will reduce to make a thick, curdled sauce.
10. Carefully remove the chicken from the oven, slice the chicken and serve.

Photo Page 84

BEATEN LAMB CUTLETS

Ingredients:

16 lamb chops
3 tablespoons extra-virgin olive oil, for brushing
sea salt and freshly ground black pepper
2 lemons, halved, to serve

Serves 4

Equipment:

scale
measuring spoons
sharp knife
mallet or rolling pin
pastry brush
large frying pan
tongs

These lamb chops can be eaten with your hands. The thinner you can make them the better. They are also good grilled on the barbecue.

1. Trim all the fat from the chops.
2. Using a mallet or a rolling pin, carefully press to flatten out the meat as thin as you can. Once flattened, each lamb chop should be twice its original width.
3. Brush each chop on both sides with olive oil and season well with salt and pepper.
4. Heat a large frying pan over a high heat.
5. Working in batches, lay the chops side by side in the pan.
6. Fry over a high heat for 2 minutes to brown.
7. Turn over the chops with tongs and fry on the other side for 2 minutes.
8. Repeat for the remaining chops until they are all cooked.
9. Serve the chops in a pile with lemon halves. Eat with your fingers while still warm.

Photo Page 86

STEAK

Ingredients:

2 x (250g/9 oz) sirloin (short loin) steaks,
about 6cm (2½ inches) thick
sea salt and freshly ground black pepper
extra-virgin olive oil, for drizzling

Serves 2

Equipment:

scale
barbecue, griddle (grill) pan or grill (broiler)
tongs
sharp knife

The trick here is to have the confidence to leave the steaks on the grill for the full cooking time. It means that it will get the lovely griddled markings. Also be sure to rest your meat, which makes it juicier and more flavourful.

1. About 30 minutes before cooking, remove the steaks from the refrigerator, uncovered, and let them come to room temperature.
2. Preheat a barbecue, griddle (grill) pan or grill (broiler) to high heat.
3. Season the steaks on both sides with salt and pepper.
4. Reduce the heat to medium. Grill the steaks on one side for 3 minutes.
5. Turn over the steaks with tongs and grill for 2–3 minutes on the other side.
6. Put the steaks onto a plate.
7. Let them rest somewhere warm for 5 minutes.
8. Slice the steaks thickly on the diagonal, then drizzle with olive oil.

Photo Page 89

ARISTA DI MAIALE

Ingredients:

2 sprigs rosemary, leaves picked
4 cloves garlic
sea salt and freshly ground black pepper
1.5kg (3lb 5 oz) pork loin on the bone
4 tablespoons extra-virgin olive oil

Serves 6

Equipment:

scale
measuring spoons
sharp knife
roasting tin (pan)
oven gloves

This recipe is lovely if you get creative with using herbs. Fennel seeds taste great with pork as a classic combination – just add with the rosemary.

1. Preheat the oven to 180°C/Gas Mark 4 (350°F).
2. Chop the rosemary and garlic together with 1 tablespoon of salt.
3. Rub the rosemary mixture all over the meat.
4. Put the loin in a roasting tin (pan) and drizzle with the olive oil.
5. Roast in the oven for 1 hour 30 minutes, turning the meat over from time to time.
6. Halfway through, add 3 tablespoons of water to the pan to loosen the juices.
7. Carefully remove from the oven. Put somewhere warm and allow the meat to rest for 5 minutes.
8. Thickly slice the loin.
9. Serve with the concentrated juices from the pan.

Photo Page 91

DOLCI

ALMOND MERINGUE WITH STRAWBERRIES

Ingredients:

Meringue
110g (1 stick/½ cup) butter, melted, plus extra for greasing
5 large (extra-large) egg whites
225g (1 cup plus 1½ tablespoons) caster (superfine) sugar (divided)
175g (1¼ cups) ground almonds
70g (scant ½ cup) plain (all-purpose) flour

Strawberries and cream
1 vanilla pod (bean)
1 litre (34 fl oz/4¼ cups) double (heavy) cream
150g (1 cup plus 3 tablespoons) icing (confectioners') sugar
1.5kg (3¼ quarts) strawberries, hulled and halved

Serves 10

Equipment:

scale
measuring cups
measuring spoons
sharp knife
baking sheets
baking (parchment) paper
2 bowls
electric whisk
spoon
sieve
wire racks
whisk
plate or cake stand
flat-bladed knife

When separating the eggs, be sure there is no yellow in the whites. To test if you've beaten the eggs stiff enough you should be able to hold the bowl upside down.

1. Preheat the oven to 120°C/Gas Mark ½ (250°F).
2. Grease three baking sheets, line with baking (parchment) paper, then grease the paper.
3. Put the egg whites and half of the sugar in a bowl and beat with an electric whisk until stiff peaks form.
4. Add the ground almonds and the remaining sugar, then briefly beat to mix.
5. Fold in the melted butter using a spoon.
6. Finally, sift the flour into the bowl and carefully fold in.
7. Divide the mixture equally between the three trays and spread it out flat and as thin as you can: 1 cm (½ inch) thick at most.
8. Bake in the oven for 50 minutes, or until set and nearly crisp.
9. While the meringues are hot, carefully peel off the baking paper.
10. Cool the meringues on wire racks.
11. Halve the vanilla pod (bean) and scrape out the seeds.
12. Put the cream, vanilla seeds and icing (confectioners') sugar in a bowl and lightly whip using a whisk.
13. Put the first meringue layer on a large, flat plate or cake stand.
14. Using a flat-bladed knife, cover with one-third of the cream, then top with one-third of the strawberry halves.
15. Repeat twice.

Photo Page 92

LEMON ICE CREAM

Ingredients:

finely grated zest of 1 and juice of 3 lemons
200g (1 cup) caster (superfine) sugar
½ teaspoon sea salt
450ml (15 fl oz/scant 2 cups) double (heavy) cream

Serves 6

Equipment:

lemon squeezer
grater
scale
measuring cups
measuring spoons
bowl
spoon
freezer-proof container

This is the only ice cream we know that doesn't have to be churned. Be sure to wash the lemons. Roll the lemons before you squeeze them to get the maximum juice.

1. In a bowl, mix the lemon zest and juice, sugar and salt with a spoon.
2. Slowly add the cream, carefully mixing with the spoon: it will immediately thicken.
3. Put the ice-cream mixture in a 1-litre (1-quart) freezer-proof container and freeze for 2 hours to harden.

Photo Page 95

RASPBERRY SORBET

Ingredients:

1 thick-skinned lemon
400g (2 cups) caster (superfine) sugar
800g (4½ cups) raspberries

Serves 6

Equipment:

scale
measuring cups
sharp knife
food processor
freezer-proof container
spoon

The riper the raspberries, the better the sorbet.

1. Cut the lemon into 1-cm (½-inch) cubes, removing any pips (seeds).
2. Put the lemon into a food processor with 350g (1¾ cups) of the caster (superfine) sugar.
3. Blend until puréed with visible bits of lemon skin.
4. Add the raspberries, then blend again until well mixed.
5. Pour the mixture into a freezer-proof container and freeze for about 2 hours, stirring with a spoon to break up the crystals every 30 minutes, until solid.

Photo Page 97

HAZELNUT PRALINE SEMIFREDDO

Ingredients:

Praline
olive oil, for greasing
300g (1⅞ cups) blanched hazelnuts
225g (1 cup plus 1½ tablespoons)
caster (superfine) sugar

Semifreddo
900ml (30 fl oz/3¾ cups) milk
650ml (22 fl oz/2¾ cups)
double (heavy) cream (divided)
8 large (extra-large) egg yolks
175g (⅞ cup) caster (superfine) sugar

Serves 6

Equipment:

scale
measuring cups
baking (parchment) paper
baking sheet
saucepan
wooden spoon
rolling pin
food processor
heavy saucepan
2 bowls
whisk
freezer-proof container

If you want to skip the first three steps, it's easier to use peeled hazelnuts. Be careful when you are making the caramel - it will be extremely hot.

1. To make the praline, preheat the oven to 200°C/Gas Mark 6 (400°F). Line a baking sheet with baking (parchment) paper. Grease the paper.
2. Add the nuts to the prepared baking sheet.
3. Roast in the oven for 4–5 minutes until golden brown. Set aside to cool.
4. Put the sugar and 150ml (5 fl oz/⅔ cup) water in a saucepan and bring to the boil.
5. Cook for 8–10 minutes until it turns into a dark caramel.
6. Ask an adult to help pour the caramel over the nuts.
7. Leave to cool until solid. This is your praline. Break it up.
8. Put the praline in a food processor and break up as finely as possible.
9. To make the semifreddo, in a heavy saucepan, combine the milk and 300ml (10 fl oz/1¼ cups) cream.
10. Heat over a high heat until almost boiling, then remove from the heat.
11. Whisk the egg yolks and sugar in a bowl for about 5 minutes until pale.
12. Mix a cup of the hot cream mixture into the egg yolks with the whisk.
13. Transfer the whole lot back into the pan.
14. Stir over a low heat for 10–15 minutes until the mixture has thickened.
15. Pour into a bowl and leave to cool. This is your semifreddo.
16. Stir the praline powder into the cooled semifreddo mixture.
17. Transfer to a 2-litre (2-quart) freezer-proof container and freeze for 1 hour 30 minutes.
18. In a bowl, lightly beat the remaining 350ml (12fl oz/11/2 cups) of the cream to form soft peaks.
19. Mix the cream into the semifreddo and freeze for 1 hour.

Photo Page 99

PRESSED CHOCOLATE CAKE

Ingredients:

300g (2½ sticks plus 1 tablespoon/ generous 1¼ cups) butter, plus extra for greasing
plain (all-purpose) flour, for dusting
400g (14 oz) chocolate
80g (⅔ cup) cocoa powder, sifted
10 medium (large) eggs, separated
225g (1 cup plus 1½ tablespoons) caster (superfine) sugar (divided)

Serves 6

Equipment:

scale
measuring cups
measuring spoons
sieve
cake tin
saucepan
heatproof bowl
wooden spoon
bowl
metal spoon
whisk
oven gloves
baking (parchment) paper
plate
heavy weights

It sounds eccentric, but pressing the cake down is what makes this cake special. It's delicious with vanilla ice cream.

1. Preheat the oven to 180°C/Gas Mark 4 (350°F).
2. Butter and flour a 30-cm (12-inch) round cake tin (pan), about 7.5cm (3 inches) deep.
3. Bring a saucepan filled halfway with water to the boil.
4. Reduce the heat to a simmer.
5. Set a heatproof bowl over the saucepan; the water should not touch the bowl.
6. Add the butter, chocolate and cocoa to the bowl and mix until melted.
7. Carefully place the bowl on the work counter and leave to cool for 10 minutes.
8. In a bowl, whisk the egg yolks with half the sugar until pale and thick.
9. Stir this gently into the cooled chocolate mixture with a metal spoon.
10. In a clean bowl, beat the egg whites with the other half of the sugar until they form soft peaks.
11. One-third at a time, fold the egg whites gently into the chocolate mixture with the spoon.
12. Pour the mixture into the prepared cake tin.
13. Bake in the oven for 25–30 minutes until the cake has risen.
14. Carefully remove from the oven.
15. Immediately top with a square of baking (parchment) paper and a plate that fits 1 cm (½ inch) inside the rim.
16. Press down firmly, then put a weight on top to squash the cake a little.
17. Allow the cake to cool fully before turning it out.

Photo Page 100

CROSTATA

Ingredients:

Raspberry jam
450g (2½ cups) raspberries
225g (1 cup plus 1½ tablespoons) caster (superfine) sugar
juice of 1 large lemon

Pastry (pie) dough
250g (1⅔ cups) plain (all-purpose) flour, plus extra for dusting
3½ tablespoons caster (superfine) sugar
2½ tablespoons polenta (cornmeal)
1 teaspoon salt
170g (1½ sticks/¾ cup) butter, cold and diced
1 egg, beaten
1 tablespoon demerara (turbinado) sugar, for sprinkling

Serves 6

Equipment:

scale
measuring cups
measuring spoons
large frying pan
wooden spoon
bowl
stand mixer fitted with a paddle attachment
clingfilm (plastic wrap)
rolling pin
tart pan
pasta cutter
baking (parchment) paper
blunt knife
pastry brush

You can use any jam you like (even ready-made) with this tart, but if making it yourself, it can get extremely hot, so take care.

1. To make the raspberry jam, combine all the ingredients in a large frying pan.
2. Bring to the boil over a medium heat. Stir frequently to dissolve the sugar.
3. Increase the heat and boil for 5 minutes.
4. Carefully pour the mixture into a bowl and cool completely.
5. To make the pastry, in a stand mixer fitted with the paddle attachment, combine flour, caster sugar, polenta (cornmeal), salt and butter.
6. Beat on a low speed until butter is reduced to pea-sized chunks.
7. Add 4 tablespoons of iced water and mix until combined.
8. Cover the dough with the clingfilm and chill in the refrigerator for 1 hour.
9. Divide the dough in half. Using a rolling pin, roll a piece of dough on a lightly floured work counter, slightly larger than your tart pan and to a thickness of 3 mm (⅛ inch).
10. Carefully lay the dough over the tart pan. Set aside.
11. Roll the other piece of dough into a rectangle the width of the tart.
12. Using a pasta cutter, cut 8 strips, about 2.5-cm (1-inch) wide. Create a 4 × 4 lattice on a piece of baking (parchment) paper.
13. Preheat the oven to 160°C/Gas Mark 3 (325°F).
14. Fill the pastry with raspberry jam.
15. Carefully slide the lattice on top. Using a blunt knife, trim the edges.
16. Brush with the beaten egg.
17. Sprinkle with demerara (turbinado) sugar.
18. Bake for 1 hour until cooked through. Carefully remove from the oven and set aside to cool.

Photo Page 102

CHOCOLATE TRUFFLES

Ingredients:

150ml (5 fl oz/⅔ cup) double (heavy) cream
400g (14 oz) dark (semisweet) chocolate, broken into small pieces
5 tablespoons butter, softened
6 tablespoons best-quality unsweetened cocoa powder

Makes 25 truffles

Equipment:

measuring cups
saucepan
wooden spoon
large plate
small plate
jug
teaspoon

Keep the spoon you're going to use for the curling in a jug of warm water.

1. Pour the cream into a pan and bring to the boil.
2. Boil the cream over a high heat until it reduces to 2 tablespoons.
3. Remove from the heat.
4. Add the chocolate and stir in with a spoon until melted.
5. Add the butter and stir gently.
6. Pour the mixture onto a large plate.
7. Chill in the refrigerator for about 45 minutes until set.
8. Sprinkle the cocoa powder over a small plate.
9. With a teaspoon, scrape across the chocolate to form a rough sphere; it should be a curl, not a ball.
10. Roll in the cocoa powder.
11. Repeat the last two steps until all the mixture is shaped.
12. Chill the truffles in the refrigerator for at least 30 minutes before serving.

Photo Page 105

PISTACHIO CAKE

Ingredients:

120g (¾ cup) pistachios
5 tablespoons blanched almonds
250g (2¼ sticks/1 cup plus 2 tablespoons) butter, plus extra for greasing
250g (1¼ cups) caster (superfine) sugar
grated zest and juice of 1 lemon
1 vanilla pod (bean), sliced lengthways
4 eggs
100g (⅔ cup) plain (all-purpose) flour
½ teaspoon baking powder
pinch of salt

Topping
50g (¼ cup) caster (superfine) sugar
grated zest and juice of 1 lemon
60g (⅓ cup plus 1 tablespoon) pistachios, finely chopped

Serves 6

Equipment:

scale
measuring cups
measuring spoons
grater
lemon juicer
loaf tin (pan)
baking (parchment) paper
food processor
bowl
wooden spoon
sharp knife
electric mixer
skewer
oven gloves
small saucepan

Use high-quality shelled pistachios and your cake will come out a beautiful green colour.

1. Preheat the oven to 150°C/Gas Mark 2 (300°F).
2. Line a loaf tin (pan) with baking (parchment) paper.
3. In a food processor, finely grind the pistachios and almonds.
4. In a separate bowl, combine the butter, sugar and lemon juice and zest.
5. Scrape the seeds of the vanilla pod (bean) into bowl.
6. Using an electric mixer, beat for 5 minutes until pale and fluffy.
7. Add the eggs one by one, mixing well between each addition.
8. Add the ground nuts, flour, baking powder and salt.
   Using a wooden spoon, mix until well combined.
9. Pour the batter into the prepared loaf tin.
10. Carefully put tin in the oven.
11. Bake for 1 hour, or until golden brown and a skewer inserted into the centre comes out clean. Carefully remove the cake.
12. Meanwhile, combine sugar and lemon juice and zest in a small saucepan.
    Stir gently over a low heat until sugar dissolves to create a syrup.
13. Sprinkle the pistachios in a long row over the cake.
    Pour the warm lemon syrup on top.
14. Set aside to cool.
15. Remove from the pan and serve.

Photo Page 107

PEAR AND ALMOND TART

Ingredients:

Pastry (pie) dough
350g (2¼ cups) plain (all-purpose) flour
pinch of salt
100g (¾ cup) icing (confectioners') sugar
225g (2 sticks/1 cup) cold butter,
cut into cubes
3 medium (large) egg yolks

Filling
350g (3 sticks/1½ cups) butter, softened
350g (1¾ cups) caster (superfine) sugar
350g (3 cups) ground almonds
(almond meal)
3 medium (large) eggs
6 ripe Doyenne du Comice (Comice) pears

Serves 10

Equipment:

scale
measuring cups
measuring spoons
food processor
clingfilm (plastic wrap)
grater
tart tin
bowl
wooden spoon
vegetable peeler
small knife
oven gloves

The nuts must be finely ground to create the light-textured filling.

1. To make the pastry, put the flour, salt, sugar and butter in a food processor.
2. Pulse for 1 minute until the mixture resembles coarse breadcrumbs.
3. Add the egg yolks and pulse 6 times until the mixture comes together and leaves the sides of the bowl.
4. Remove the mixture from the food processor.
5. Wrap in clingfilm (plastic wrap) and chill in the refrigerator for at least 1 hour.
6. Preheat the oven to 180°C/Gas Mark 4 (350°F).
7. Coarsely grate (shred) the pastry (dough) into a 30-cm (12-inch) loose-bottomed, fluted flan tin (quiche pan).
8. Press the grated pastry (dough) evenly on the sides and base.
9. Bake in the oven for 20 minutes until very light brown.
10. Carefully remove from the oven.
11. Leave to cool to room temperature.
12. Reduce the oven temperature to 150°C/Gas Mark 2 (300°F).
13. To make the filling, in a bowl, cream the butter and sugar with a wooden spoon until the mixture is pale and light.
14. Mix in the ground almonds, then beat in the eggs one by one.
15. Spoon the filling into the cooled pastry (pie) shell.
16. Peel, halve and core the pears.
17. Arrange the pears over the frangipane filling.
18. Bake in the oven for 1 hour 30 minutes, or until golden brown.
19. Carefully remove from the oven and serve.

Photo Page 108

RICCIARELLI

Ingredients:

2–3 (75g/2¾ oz) egg whites
dash of lemon juice
220g (1⅔ cups) icing (confectioners') sugar,
plus extra for rolling
435g (3½ cups) ground almonds
(almond meal)
pinch of salt
grated zest of 2 oranges

Makes 36 biscuits (cookies)

Equipment:

scale
measuring cups
bowl
whisk
metal spoon
knife
baking sheet
baking (parchment) paper

It's best to eat these right away as they don't last long and will lose their chewiness.

1. In a bowl, whisk the egg whites with the lemon juice until soft peaks form.
2. A little at a time, whisk in the icing (confectioners') sugar until the mixture is shiny and stiff.
3. Fold in the ground almonds, salt and orange zest with a metal spoon. Work gently so you do not deflate the mixture.
4. Chill the dough in the refrigerator for 30 minutes.
5. Preheat the oven to 160°C/Gas Mark 3 (325°F).
6. Generously dust a work counter with icing sugar.
7. Using your hands, roll a handful of the dough into a soft cylinder, 6cm (2½ inches) thick.
8. Cut into 1-cm ((½-inch)-thick slices and roll them in more icing sugar.
9. Repeat the last two steps for the remaining batter.
10. Place the biscuits on a baking sheet lined with baking (parchment) paper.
11. Bake in the oven for 20 minutes.

Photo Page 111

1. All spoon and cup measurements are level, unless otherwise stated. 1 teaspoon = 5 ml; 1 tablespoon = 15 ml. Australian standard tablespoons are 20 ml, so Australian readers are advised to use 3 teaspoons in place of 1 tablespoon when measuring small quantities.
2. We always use unsalted butter.
3. Eggs to be medium (large in the US).
4. Sugar is white caster (superfine) sugar and brown sugar is cane or demerara (turbinado) unless otherwise specified.
5. Cream is 36–40% fat heavy whipping cream.
6. Milk is full-fat (whole) and homogenized.
7. Cooking times are for guidance only, as individual ovens vary. If using a conventional oven, follow the manufacturer's instructions concerning oven temperatures.
8. Exercise a high level of caution when following recipes involving any potentially hazardous activity, including the use of high temperatures, open flames and when frying.
9. Both metric and imperial measures are used in this book. Follow one set of measurements throughout, not a mixture, as they are not interchangeable.

NOTES

INDEX

ACKNOWLEDGEMENTS

Emma Collier
Eliza Dolbey
Jessica Filbey
Charlotte Grocutt
Roger Guyett
Anna Higham
Georgia Kirsop
Lèonie McQuillan
Michelle Meade
Caroline Michel
Alex Owens
Holly Pollard
Nina Raine
Claire Rogers
Carlota Soper
Emilia Terragni
Matilda Trivelli
Maude Tisch
Annabella Tubbs
Jemi Vilhena
Vashti Armit
Charles Pullan
Debra Black
and everyone at
The River Café

Design:
Anthony Michael and
Stephanie Nash at
Michael Nash Associates

Phaidon Press Limited
2 Cooperage Yard
London E15 2QR

Phaidon Press Inc.
65 Bleecker Street
New York, NY 10012

phaidon.com

First published in 2022

ISBN 978 1 83866 445 9
ISBN 978 1 83866 531 9 (signed edition)

A CIP catalogue record for this book is
available from the the British Library
and the Library of Congress.

Commissioning Editor:
Emilia Terragni

Project Editor:
Ellie Smith

Production Controller:
Gif Jittiwutikarn

Photography:
Matthew Donaldson

Printed in Italy

The publisher would like to thank
Michelle Meade, João Mota, Elizabeth
Parson, Holly Pollard, Claire Rogers,
Tracey Smith, Kathy Steer, Hans Stofregen
for their contributions to the book.